OXFORD
INDIA SHORT
INTRODUCTIONS

CITIZENSHIP IN INDIA

The Oxford India Short
Introductions are concise,
stimulating, and accessible guides
to different aspects of India.
Combining authoritative analysis,
new ideas, and diverse perspectives,
they discuss subjects which are
topical yet enduring, as also
emerging areas of study and debate.

OTHER TITLES IN THE SERIES

Capital Flows and Exchange Rate Management
Soumyen Sikdar

Trade and Environment
Rajat Acharyya

Dalit Assertion
Sudha Pai

Political Economy of Reforms in India
Rahul Mukherji

Coalition Politics in India
Bidyut Chakrabarty

Mughal Painting
S.P. Verma

Pathways to Economic Development
Amitava K. Dutta

International Trade and India
Parthapratim Pal

Indian Foreign Policy
Sumit Ganguly

The Indian Middle Class
Surinder S. Jodhka and Aseem Prakash

Labour in Contemporary India
Praveen Jha

Bollywood
M.K. Raghavendra

For more information visit our website:
https://india.oup.com/content/series/o/
oxford-india-short-introductions/

OXFORD
INDIA SHORT
INTRODUCTIONS

CITIZENSHIP
IN INDIA

ANUPAMA ROY

OXFORD
UNIVERSITY PRESS

OXFORD
UNIVERSITY PRESS

Oxford University Press is a department of the University of Oxford.
It furthers the University's objective of excellence in research, scholarship,
and education by publishing worldwide. Oxford is a registered trademark of
Oxford University Press in the UK and in certain other countries.

Published in India by
Oxford University Press
YMCA Library Building, 1 Jai Singh Road, New Delhi 110 001, India

ISBN-13: 978-0-19-946796-9
ISBN-10: 0-19-946796-X

Typeset in 11/15.6 Bembo Std
by Excellent Laser Typesetters, Pitampura, Delhi 110 034
Printed in India by Replika Press Pvt. Ltd

Chapter 2 of this volume is a revised version of 'The Nation and its "Constitution":
The Text and Context of Citizenship' that appeared in *Gendered Citizenship: Historical
and Conceptual Explorations* published by Orient Blackswan. © 2005 Orient Blackswan
Private Limited.

Contents

Acknowledgements

It is with deep affection and gratitude that I acknowledge the help and assistance I received over the past one year, while writing this book and preparing it for publication. I am grateful to my family for their selfless and unwavering love, to my friends for making time for me, and to my colleagues at the Centre for Political Studies in Jawaharlal Nehru University for their support and encouragement. I have benefited from the comments and suggestions that have been made to my presentations in various conferences. I appreciate the feedback I received from the two referees. I would also like to thank Oxford University Press, Delhi, for inviting me to write this book, which gave me the opportunity to revisit and build upon my earlier work.

Acknowledgements

Introduction
Landscapes of Citizenship

I know of at least one fellow called Ramu whose house was in the proximity of an election-meetings ground. It was great entertainment for him while it lasted.... On the eve of voting, Ramu and his friends spent long hours not only in vigorous demonstrations but also in excited discussion.

'My father has promised to take me too for voting', said one.

'Nonsense. We won't be allowed to go there; it is only for grown-ups.'

'… It seems anyone can vote, didn't you hear what they said in the meetings?'

'Not everybody, only tall persons will be allowed to vote.'

'No. It is all wrong. What about our geography master? He is our height and I know he is going to vote.'

'What is a vote like?'

'My father said it is made of paper.'

'What is its shape?'

'We are not allowed to see it'.

'I am going to slip in somehow and see what it is like. They are going to have it after all in our school ...'

'You will be handcuffed if you go there, it is against the law to try and see the vote. Don't you see how many police they have kept there?'.... Needless to say when the elders went out to cast their votes, they left the children behind much to their chagrin, which increased when the elders came back and displayed the little dot on their fingers. It made a little girl Kamala very jealous, and she vowed, 'See if I don't get my vote very soon. And when they put that dot on I will tell them to place it between my eyebrows... ' (Narayan 2000: 291–2).

Writing about the first general election in India in a short story titled 'The Election Game', R.K. Narayan recounts the election fever that seized the people participating in what he called 'a large scale rehearsal for political life'. No one, young or old, was left untouched, 'as though a sense of sovereignty [was] aroused even in the most insignificant of us' (Narayan 1952). The children too had adopted electioneering as one of their games. This fictional rendition of the first general election reflects not only the enigma surrounding it, but also its historical and political significance. The exercise of franchise was an unfamiliar experience for the large numbers of hitherto colonial subjects deprived of political rights. Elections embodied the fundamental rupture that independence from colonial rule was to bring in its wake, affirming the powerful imaginary of a sovereign nation of citizens. Central to this imaginary was the creation of a political community of citizens and a democratic public sphere. The exercise of *universal* adult suffrage, which substituted the colonial practice of limited franchise restricted by property and education criteria, was a manifestation of political equality, and the promise that government was to be based on principles of popular sovereignty and self-determination expressed through representative institutions.

Elections mark moments in politics when power is democratized by making the government subject to the consent of the governed. In order to ensure that this consent has not been elicited through coercion, elections are conducted by following procedures that make the unfettered exercise of both the individual and the collective act of voting possible. The right to vote along with the right to contest elections and the right to form associations and unions are important components of citizenship. The emergence of political rights has been an integral part of the history of the development of modern citizenship as a condition of expanding equality, supplanting the rigid hierarchies of societies based on ascriptive status. However, while important for affirming equal citizenship, political enfranchisement alone does not constitute democratic citizenship.

Citizens are members of the political community and all those who have the status of citizens are bearers of equal civil, political, and social rights. This commonly accepted definition of citizenship made influential by the British sociologist T.H. Marshall (1950) holds out the promise of equality and integration within the political community. A *political* community is distinct from ascriptive communities, which may be based on ties of birth, kinship, caste, religion, and the like. A political community comes into existence when people agree to live together within a framework of mutually agreed and recognized rules, consenting to give to a sovereign political authority the power to enforce these rules, the consent being subject to periodic renewal, with the people retaining the power to withdraw it. The emergence of citizenship as a camaraderie of equals is an outcome of past and ongoing struggles around the expansion of specific rights (for example, the right to vote), the making of collective national identities (for example, through anti-colonial movements), and in transitions from authoritarian to democratic governments (for example, the post-apartheid regime in South Africa).

More often than not, citizenship is seen in terms of a legal/formal status: having a nationality and being a member of a nation state, and deriving from this status, rights guaranteed and protected by the constitution, and duties and responsibilities laid down by it. The idea of citizenship, however, goes beyond legal or formal membership to concerns around substantive membership and terms of belonging. Substantive membership refers to questions pertaining to socio-economic inequalities based on class, caste, gender, race, ethnicity, sexuality, and the like. While citizenship is identified with an ideal condition of equality, it may actually remain elusive and fettered, since societies are characterized by hierarchies and inequalities rather than equality and belonging. In addition, citizenship itself produces hierarchies by laying down terms of inclusion that make themselves manifest through two parallel and mutually contradictory processes—*masking* and *marking*. In order to be a status shared in common by all, citizenship demands an abstraction, which assumes a privileged status of dissociation, not available in an equal measure to all. In other words, in order to become an equal member of the political community, a citizen is required to disengage herself/himself from all constitutive social contexts like caste, class, religion, gender, sexuality, and the like, to present herself/himself as a masked citizen. On the other hand, citizenship also involves a process of *marking* of citizens in particular ways so that they are either not citizens at all or are citizens of particular types. For example, the power to dissociate from and thereby mask one's social identity to enter the world of unmarked citizens with equal rights may not be available to Dalit women whose bodies are indelibly marked by caste and gender. Indeed, the process of masking and marking are at the core of the paradox of inequality inherent in citizenship.

Equality as an integral component of citizenship, however, gives it its unique character as a 'momentum concept' (Hoffman 2004) with a liberatory promise. This basically means that when understood as a condition of equality, drawing from what is seen and experienced as fair, equal, and just terms of belonging, citizenship may be construed as a condition worth striving for. In a social context replete with inequalities, citizenship may well become a terrain of contest and struggle, where a multitude of social and political forces and ideological formulations exist in conflicting relationships. As an idea inspiring struggle, and on the other hand as a process whereby citizens are legally constituted in specific historical settings through the interplay of social and institutional power, citizenship remains a condition that is unbounded, changing, and always incomplete. It needs to continually respond to new contexts and present itself through new idioms and languages emerging from people's practices of citizenship. Conversely, it is also steeped in the language of rule and order, which comes from the state practices of governing.

In an eloquently written essay on 'essentially contested concepts' published in the 1950s, W.B. Gallie proposed that concepts are informed by endless disputes about their appropriate *usage*. While there may be triumphal moments for a specific usage, the sides arrayed in the dispute continually claim coequality, which could make either, or both of them, concurrently, as well as potentially, champion arguments. Irrespective of the validity of their respective claims to ascendancy, disputes around a concept prepare the ground for philosophical enquiry, opening it up for elucidation and scrutiny. This scrutiny pertains in particular to the explanations it offers and the analytical tools it supplies for studying particular social and political experiences. Around the same time that Gallie was writing about the contests that inhere in concepts, Lloyd and Susanne Rudolph (1958) were on a field visit to India to study the second general election in a country where the exercise of franchise and participation in the electoral process was not yet a 'familiar' experience. The Rudolphs realized, and stressed emphatically in an article published subsequently, that modes of enquiry that were developed in a particular context could not be transferred elsewhere on an assumption of universal applicability. Indeed, they found the tools developed in the 'familiar' contexts of American politics not only appear 'strange' in the Indian context, but also completely inadequate and ineffective in making intelligible the evolving contours of electoral democracy in India. Not surprisingly, the article stressed the need for devising conceptual tools that were not simply efficient, but also intelligible, an attribute that does not refer to their application in the same form across cultures, but to their mobility and the capacity to assume legible forms as they travelled.

Taking a cue from Gallie, and Lloyd and Susanne Rudolph, one may begin from the premise that citizenship is an essentially contested concept, and as such is capable of both garnering and generating a range of meanings, which make it intelligible in specific contexts. The question of intelligibility is of course a complex one. In order for something to be intelligible, it needs to be inserted in a shared code of meanings. These meanings are likely to make things comprehensible, but in specific ways. For example, a podium in a classroom may be perceived as the location from which the teacher is likely to speak to her class, placed in a chapel it identifies the space from which the priest will deliver a sermon, in a public hall it is the point from which a persuasive exhortation is made, and in a furniture shop it is a commodity that may be bought to be put to any of these uses. Thus, the question of intelligibility needs to be understood in terms of the meanings a concept may assume and convey within a distinct set of historically situated social relations.

Over the past several years, the understanding of citizenship has no longer been limited to a political and juridical status within territorially inscribed nation states, and the entitlements that this status brings. Studies of citizenship have taken what may be called an anthropological turn, meandering along sites that are heterogeneous, speaking of citizenship practices beyond political engagements with the state, inflected by both the plurality of its idioms and mutations in its practices. The collection of articles in a recent issue of the journal *Citizenship Studies*, for example, draws attention to the 'distinctive capacity' of citizenship to connect diverse settings, struggles, and strategies. For the editors of the issue, citizenship can be grasped as a powerful keyword in political, social, and cultural terms that designates possible, actual, or desired relationships. However, as a keyword, they argue, citizenship can only be a 'connecting' idea, though not a universal one (Neveu et al. 2011). While agreeing with this framework, it may however be argued that plurality of idioms, diversity of scales and sites, and mutations in practices assume significance not in discrete and disparate existence, but within a referential framework, informed by meanings that lay claims to universality. Thus, if one were to understand citizenship as a connecting idea, through its plural expressions in time, and mutations in practices across time, it may perhaps be worthwhile to see it as polyrhythmous rather than heterogeneous.

What do I mean by polyrhythms? History, says Elsa Barkley-Brown, is like music, where everybody is talking at once, with multiple rhythms being played simultaneously. Events and people that get written about, she argues, '[do] not occur in isolation but in dialogue with a myriad of other people and events', so that at 'any given moment millions of people are all talking at once' (Barkley-Brown 1991: 85). The historian isolates one conversation to explore, but puts it in a context, in order to make evident its dialogue with several other related conversations. The idea is to make the isolated lyric stand alone, but at the same time be in connection with all the other lyrics being sung. The task of studying citizenship involves a similar craft of extricating and isolating distinctive strands from the multiple lyrics being sung simultaneously, and steering them back into their polyrhythmous location so that one can see the relationship between them. This process of extraction, isolation, and subsequent relocation is integral to the quest for familiarity and intelligibility, that is, rolling back of estrangement from citizenship. Making citizenship familiar entails making the strange comprehensible in its polyrhythmous variations, but more importantly, it involves a process of inversion, in which the familiar assumes a different meaning altogether.

Scholars who have written on citizenship have held diverse and often divergent views on both its meaning and usage, prompting the suggestion that citizenship is a contested concept. At one end of the spectrum of the scholarship on citizenship are scholars who look at citizenship as a 'momentum' concept (Hoffman 2004). Unlike 'static' concepts like patriarchy and violence, all of which are repressively hierarchical and oppressive, as a momentum concept citizenship is seen as having an inherent logic and historical dynamic which makes it progressively universal and egalitarian (Hoffman 2004). These frameworks see citizenship as having an impetus and propulsion towards universality, that is, the capacity to extend and deepen itself, and change its content, to bring increasing numbers of people into its fold. The idea of citizenship as a continuous movement towards equality and universality may be found in T.H. Marshall's lecture on 'Citizenship and Social Class' delivered in Cambridge in February 1949. In his lecture, Marshall presented a paradigm for explaining the development of citizenship in England from the eighteenth to the twentieth century as a process of expanding equality against the inequality of social class, in a peculiar relationship of conflict and collusion with capitalism. Marshall identified three constituent elements of citizenship, namely, civil, political, and social, and traced their development alongside the emergence of specific state structures and institutions. He described this development as a process of '*continuous progress* for some two hundred and fifty years' (Marshall 1950: 10; emphasis added). The definition of citizenship as 'full and equal membership in the political community', attributed to Marshall, has been inferred from the following:

> Citizenship is a status bestowed on those who are full members of a community. All who possess the status are equal with respect to the rights and duties with which the status is endowed. There is no universal principle that determines what those rights and duties shall be, but societies in which citizenship is a developing institution create an image of an ideal citizenship against which achievement can be measured and towards which aspiration can be directed. (Marshall 1950: 28–9)

Evidently, in Marshall's framework, citizenship is a status of full membership, and all those who have such a status are equal with respect to their entitlement to rights and obligations. It may, therefore, be assumed that the *camaraderie* of equals, which citizenship ushers in, is dependent on a prior status of membership, and the distinction, therefore, between citizens and non-citizens. The association of citizenship with legal status may be seen as a continuing legacy of the passive citizenship of absolutist states concerned with imposing their authority over heterogeneous populations.

Yet, the passivity of status is ruptured by the dynamism implicit in the image of an ideal citizenship towards which aspirations for citizenship are directed. Herein lies the promise of citizenship.

At the other end of the spectrum, however, are those scholars who consider citizenship as fraught with contests. In such frameworks, citizenship is seen as an exclusive category with rigid rules identifying insiders and outsiders, to deny membership at the threshold itself. Even among members, a host of social and economic conditions would ultimately determine the terms of inclusion and belonging. Constructing a taxonomy of citizenship based on the relative positioning of citizens along actually existing hierarchies, Upendra Baxi (2002) suggests that citizenship is a condition of hierarchical inequalities. For Baxi, there exists a large mass of excluded citizens, whom he calls 'subject', 'insurgent', and 'gendered' citizens respectively. The 'super-citizens' and 'negotiating citizens', on the other hand, are the elite comprising the privileged class of citizens who remain immune from law but simultaneously have the power to represent law enforcement as regime persecution. If the negotiating and super-citizens constitute the dominant referent for citizenship, the subject–citizens are the large majority of the impoverished population, to whom the law applies relentlessly, largely to criminalize them; insurgent citizens are those 'encountered' or subjected to custodial torture, their bodies bearing witness to the power of the state; and the gendered citizens are women, lesbigay, and transgender people, who are at the receiving end of social and state violence and discrimination. Together they comprise the teeming millions for whom citizenship remains a tantalizingly close but perennially elusive horizon.

Scholars like Etienne Balibar refer to the hierarchy of citizenship as the process of producing the 'constitutive outsiders'. For Balibar (2004), the outsider or non-citizen is an indispensable element of the citizen's identity. However, this relationship between the citizen and the outsider is not one of simple opposition or exclusion; rather, the outsider is the 'other' who exists in a relationship of forclusion with the citizen (Balibar 2004). In such a relationship, the outsider is constantly present alongside the citizen, ironically like its shadow, inextricably tied to the citizen, without, however, being able to produce itself as one. Reproduced and reinscribed continually through legal and judicial pronouncement, the 'other' cohabits the citizen's space in an uneasy relationship of incongruity.

In a significant intervention in the theory of citizenship, Iris Marion Young proposed the idea of 'differentiated citizenship'. According to her, the universal ideal of citizenship as equal rights could be made effective by incorporating members of certain groups not only as individuals but also as members of groups, their rights depending in part on the special needs that emerge from their membership in particular groups. Young argues against a notion of 'universal' citizenship, which may be based on the premise of equality as 'sameness' (Young 1989). Equality as sameness carries with it a promise of universality through extension of the same status. Universality in such a framework is defined as generality—the general as opposed to the particular, that is, what citizens have in common, in opposition to how they are different from each other. To be included in this universal notion would imply 'common' as opposed to 'different' treatment, which would imply that rules and laws will be 'blind' to difference and would apply to all in the same manner. The idea of citizenship as generality and sameness assumes a state that can be a neutral arbiter standing apart from and above social differences. It also assumes a public space as a realm characterized by a commonality of interests, not burdened by the affective issues that may be generated by 'plurality' and 'difference'. Young makes a case for a group–differentiated citizenship and a heterogeneous public. In a heterogeneous public, differences are publicly recognized and acknowledged as irreducible, the political sphere is not marked by the domination of the powerful, an attempt is made to understand perspectives different from one's own, and social policies are driven by a commitment to decide on them together. Thus, instead of masking differences through the universalization of unmarked/masked citizenship, the differentiated universal proposed by Young speaks of the salience of experiential identities. These identities become significant in interaction with others and form the basis for a democratic citizenship through collective organization, an effective voice in decision-making, and recognition of difference through special group–specific rights, in addition to those enjoyed in common with others. Group–specific differentiated rights for Young would remove the blindness of citizenship to social disadvantages, experienced on grounds of race, culture, gender, age, disability, sexuality, and the like.

Citizenship is deeply embedded in state formative practices. Fixing territorial boundaries and making its inhabitants legible are important elements of statecraft, which seek to make the citizen a stable and enumerable category, amenable to specific governmental practices. Passport regimes, for example, have historically embodied the imperative to monopolize the control over the movements of people. Documents such as driving licences, passports, voter–identity cards, etc. are commonly used forms of identification. They are, however, not primarily identity documents, but documents devised to serve other purposes. Identification practices have been significant mechanisms through which the state builds enduring relationships with its citizens. Documents like the ration card, voter–identity card, driving licence, and aadhar card enable access to specific rights and welfare benefits. The regimes of national identity systems to enumerate entire populations of nation states makes these systems more comprehensive and consequential, having ramifications for the privacy of citizens and surveillance practices by the state. In the recent years, digitalized and biometric identification systems have made identification regimes more efficient but at the same time more intrusive than the older paper-based documentation regimes, for the potential they hold out for surveillance of citizens.

Surveillance, with its diverse components, namely, tools and technologies of survey, measurement, census, monitoring, and so forth, has for long been geared towards marking and making legible what is within the purview of the state's powers of extraction and control. At the same time, however, they consolidate what lies legitimately within the competence of the state. Entrenching its powers of revenue collection, garnering military service, law enforcement, and policing, these tools have over the years become more sophisticated, specialized, differentiated, and increasingly more nebulous. Interestingly, whether posited as a 'surveillance state' indicating the present specificity of the security state or in terms of 'surveillance regimes' that suggest an interlocking system of coexisting regimes, surveillance presents itself as a set of techniques as well as ideological practices for harnessing, containing, and supervising the territory and its population. Indeed, in the course of the development of these techniques the state devises novel ways of 'reaching into' society to create 'new and differentiated relationships of power', where the 'spectrum of dominance' that characterized the earlier forms of surveillance is rendered nebulous by more intangible but increasingly more penetrating technologies that significantly do not require constant proximity between the law enforcers and the people (Singh 2014: 42).

Citizenship's promise of free and equal membership in the political community, however, remains a powerful galvanizer. Increasingly, therefore, citizenship has also come to constitute a condition replete with possibilities of resistance and transformative change. Correspondingly, the social and political fields that citizenship traverses are no longer benign and impersonal or immobilized and stagnant in legal trappings. They rather signify a continually reconfiguring field of 'insurgent citizenship' (Baxi 2002; Holston 2008), informed by conflict over who belongs, how, and on what terms. It is in this unsettled/disturbed zone of contestations that new idioms and practices of citizenship are produced.

1

Who is an Indian Citizen?
The Citizenship Act of India

It is not possible to define exhaustively the conditions
of nationality, whether by birth or naturalization, by
the Constitution. If certain conditions are laid down
by the Constitution, difficulties may arise regarding the
interpretation of future legislation which may appear
to be contrary to or to depart in any way from them....
It would in our opinion, therefore, be better to specify
who would be citizens of the Indian Union at the
date when the Constitution came into force as in the
Constitution of the Irish Free State and leave the law
regarding nationality to be provided for by legislation
by the Indian Union in accordance with the accepted
principles of private international law. (Report of the
Union Constitution Committee, 26 May 1947, *Select
Documents*, pp. 577–8, cited in Rao [1968: 155])

The question 'who is an Indian citizen?' addresses the vexed issue of who can claim legal membership of India. Since Independence, the question has concerned itself with the inscription of a political entity called India, the precise demarcation of its territorial boundaries, and a template laying down the legal terms of belonging. The date of the *adoption* of the constitution, 26 November 1949, marked a crucial change in the status of the people of India. They were no longer British subjects, but citizens of the Republic of India, who derived their status as citizens from the constitution that they had enacted, adopted, and given to themselves in their collective capacity as *the people* of India. Before this, as British subjects, under the British Nationality Act, they had the status of British protected persons and not citizens.

While the word citizen is not defined in the Constitution of India, Part II of the constitution (Articles 5 to 11), titled 'Citizenship', concerned itself with the question 'Who is a citizen of India?' at the time of the *commencement* of the constitution, that is, the date on which the constitution was *adopted* by the Constituent Assembly. Although the constitution came into force only on 26 January 1950, provisions dealing with citizenship became operative on the date of its commencement, that is, 26 November 1949. The distinction between the Indian citizen and the non-citizen (alien) became effective on this date. While a citizen enjoys certain rights and is expected to perform duties that distinguish her/him from an alien, the latter has certain rights of 'personhood' that she/he possesses irrespective of the fact that she/he is not a citizen.

The constitutional provisions mention citizenship accruing on account of birth and domicile (Article 5) but also concern themselves with the modalities of addressing the complicated question of the citizenship of people 'migrating' between India and Pakistan in the course of the partition (Articles 6 and 7). Significantly, the migrant referred to by the constitution while laying down the frameworks of citizenship in the new republic was crucial to the affirmation of the sovereignty of the nation. As a consequence, the rehabilitation of the refugee, the legal accommodation of the returnee, and the recovery and rehabilitation of 'abducted' women and children—in other words, the relocation and restoration of the 'displaced' and the 'misplaced'—acquired critical significance for the invocation of citizenship.

The framing of citizenship in law may be seen as having gone through two periods of interregnum or legal hiatus. The first period of interregnum was between the formation of the Indian nation state (15 August 1947) and the enforcement of provisions of citizenship in the constitution (26 November 1949). Since the Constitution of India responded only to the context of the partition and formation of the Indian nation state, and vested the power to make laws to regulate citizenship for all future contexts in the Parliament, another period of legal vacuum ensued after November 1949 until the Citizenship Act of India was passed by the Parliament in 1955.

Tracing the Life of a Law: A Methodological Conundrum

When one reads the text of the 'bare act' of the Citizenship Act, 1955, one notices that the act comes with subtitles, each indicating successive amendments that were inserted in the original act in 1986, 1992, 2003, and 2005, up to the most recent amendment in 2015. Yet the bare act is deceptive insofar as it represents the law of citizenship in its coalescent present, compressing its different temporalities, and occluding the historical layers and flows that constitute transitions in the law. Moreover, though the points of transition are easily identifiable as specific amendments in the law, understanding the relationship between them presents a methodological challenge. Does one see each amendment as a moment of transition along a linear trajectory of 'improvement' in the law embodying a momentum towards universality; or should the transitions be seen more appropriately as uneven, made up of heterogeneous imaginaries embodying contestations around citizenship, which convey dissonance rather than consistency in its development?

A linear reading of the Citizenship Act would show that in its inaugural moment in 1955, and through subsequent amendments, the act manifested a momentum towards encompassment and progressive universality. At the same time, and paradoxically so, there can be an alternate reading, which shows the law as retreating into successive closures. Thus, if one reads the act as it existed in 1955, one notices a continuity with constitutional provisions involving procedures for the registration of displaced persons, evacuees, and returnees from Pakistan on permanent resettlement visas or entry permits, as citizens of India, and a commitment to an inclusive citizenship by birth. The 1986 amendment may well be construed as a moment of encompassment, opening up within the legal framework of citizenship a space for the articulation of difference, by responding to the concerns around citizenship in the specific context of the state of Assam. The 2003 amendment introducing the category of the 'overseas citizen of India' (OCI) may perhaps be seen as a persuasive statement of universality, embodying citizenship's contemporary moment of deterritorialized and transnational citizenship.

Yet, each of these amendments is fraught with closures so that an analogous story of hierarchical ordering through successive moments of transition may be told. In 1986, for example, the Citizenship Amendment Act put in place a system of graded citizenship in Assam, and set in motion parallel systems of identification of 'foreigners' and 'illegal migrants', deferring citizenship in some cases and attributing illegality in others. Moreover, even as the chronological boundaries of legal citizenship were shifted from 1950 to 1971 through the inscription of the Assamese exception in the citizenship law, the 1986 amendment brought another imperceptible yet significant modification in citizenship by birth. The Citizenship Act of 1955, manifesting an inclusive framework of citizenship by birth, provided that every person born in India on or after 26 January 1950, with some minor exceptions, would be a citizen of India by birth. However, from 1 July 1987, that is, the date of enforcement of the Citizenship (Amendment) Act, 1986, every person born in India could be a citizen of India only if either of her/his parents was a citizen of India at the time of her/his birth.

This change in citizenship by birth commenced a process completed with the Citizenship Amendment Act of 2003. In 2003, alongside the recognition in law of a de-territorialized, transnational/overseas Indian citizenship, the association of Indian citizenship with descent was simultaneously inscribed, as citizenship by birth became both stringent and conditional. The Amendment Act of 2003 restricted citizenship by birth to a person born in India only when both the parents were citizens of India or one parent was a citizen of India and the other was not an illegal migrant (Section 3C, Citizenship Amendment Act, 2003). The principle of *jus sanguinis*, that is, right to citizenship

7

emerging from blood ties, thus assumed primacy over the principle of *jus solis*, which is the right to citizenship associated with soil or place of birth. While the process of closure marked by the constriction of citizenship by birth began in 1986 itself, it is indeed ironic that the claims of encompassment made by overseas citizenship were synchronous with a further entrenchment of citizenship's association with descent and a closing of ranks among those born of Indian parents. It is also significant that the category 'illegal migrant' made its appearance in the legal code of citizenship simultaneously with the category 'overseas citizen', affirming the territorial and cultural closures that overseas citizenship only apparently opened.

Indeed, the law of citizenship in India may not be seen as embedded in a continuum of chronological time, but as unfolding in a sequential timeframe in which each amendment effectively puts in place a new law. The changes in the citizenship law in India, therefore, must be seen not as points in its historical evolution, but in terms of their location in a historical time-space. How is this space assembled? What are the properties that make it a historically coherent context, within which a particular amendment

8

acquires meaning? Such a reading will allow one to see the changes in the citizenship act not as a continuous historical process of evolution, but as moments punctuated by historical choices and conscious decisions. Adhering to such a framework, three decisive moments can be pinpointed in the historical trajectory of legal-formal citizenship in India: citizenship at the commencement of the Indian Republic and the enactment of the Citizenship Act of 1955, the amendment to the Citizenship Act in 1986 following the Assam Accord, and the amendment to the Citizenship Act in 2003 resulting in the insertion of the category of the OCI.

Citizenship at the Commencement of the Republic

As mentioned earlier, the Constitution of India nowhere defines the word 'citizen'. Part II of the constitution (Articles 5 to 11) titled 'Citizenship' addresses the question 'Who is a citizen of India?' at the commencement of the constitution, drawing lines between citizens and non-citizens/aliens. The demarcation of citizenship in the constitution seems to have been responding largely to, though not entirely determined by, the context of partition. Thus, even as they talk about citizenship accruing to Indians on account of birth and domicile, Articles 5 to 7 concern themselves largely with the citizenship of people 'migrating' between India and Pakistan between 1 March 1947 and 26 January 1950. The Influx from West Pakistan (Control) Ordinance came into force on 19 July 1948. Article 6 of the constitution pertains to the citizenship of persons migrating to India before and after the date on which the provisions of the Ordinance came into force. Those who came before 19 July 1948 would automatically become citizens of India, but those who came after that had to be registered by an officer on receiving an application. As far as migration from Pakistan through both its western and eastern borders was concerned, the constitution (Article 7) lays down that a person having gone to Pakistan after 1 March 1947 shall not be 'deemed to be citizen of India', unless after having migrated to Pakistan the person returned to India on a permit for resettlement. Article 8 of the constitution provides that persons residing outside India could register themselves as Indian citizens with the diplomatic or consular authority of India in that country, if they or either of their parents or grandparents were born in India (as defined in the India Act of 1935). Article 9 of the constitution, however, stipulates that no person shall be a citizen of India under Article 6 or Article 8 if he has 'voluntarily acquired the citizenship of a foreign state'. While there is no reference here to Article 7, Supreme Court judgements in the early 1960s decided that a person who migrated to Pakistan after 1 March 1947 and acquired Pakistani nationality could not claim the citizenship of India (Basu 1999: 18). Article 11 of the constitution authorized the Parliament to make laws pertaining to acquisition and termination of citizenship subsequent to the commencement of the constitution. The Citizenship Act of 1955, enacted by the Parliament, made elaborate provisions specifying how citizenship could be acquired by birth, descent, registration, naturalization, or through incorporation of territory.

Under Articles 5 to 8 of the constitution, the following categories of persons became the citizens of India at the date of the commencement of the constitution: (a) those domiciled and born in India; (b) those domiciled, not born in India but either of whose parents was born in India; (c) those domiciled, not born in India, but ordinarily resident in India for more than five years; (d) those resident in India, who migrated to Pakistan after 1 March 1947 and returned later on resettlement permits; (e) those resident in Pakistan, who migrated to India before 19 July 1948 or those who came afterwards but stayed on for more than 6 months and got registered; (f) those whose parents and grandparents were born in India but were residing outside India.

The constitutional provisions may be seen therefore as laying down the terms of citizenship for two broad categories of people: (i) those who were 'found' to be residing in India at the time of Independence and automatically became Indian citizens; (ii) those who moved across borders, a category which in turn had different patterns of movement: (a) those who migrated *from Pakistan to India* after partition and *before 19 July 1948*; (b) those who migrated *from Pakistan* to India *after 19 July 1948* but *before the commencement* of the constitution and registered themselves as citizens of India before the concerned authority; (c) those who went to Pakistan and returned to India under a permit for resettlement or permanent return issued by a competent authority.

The legal and political history of citizenship at the commencement of the Republic is tied to the history of the creation of nation states, and the drawing of borders in the Indian subcontinent. The cut-off dates and direction of movement from or into India laid down in the constitutional provisions do not capture the 'awkward' and 'ambivalent' citizens produced in the process of movement. They also do not reveal the intricate institutional responses designed to absorb or, conversely, discard those who occupied zones of liminal and indeterminate citizenship. Indeed, the two periods of interregnum comprise the legal-institutional space of possibilities, riddled and interspersed, however, with marginal and othered locations that encumber the nation state. Debates on citizenship in this period reveal cartographic anxieties over demarcating the territorial boundaries of the nation state. The processes of decision-making in disputed cases display the competing power structures emerging within the state, and the resultant accumulation and aggregation of the state power.

The partition was accompanied by an unprecedented movement of people across borders, and collective violence of an extraordinary nature,

13

including the abduction, rape, and killing of women. The governments of India and Pakistan conferred and put in place mutually agreed procedures for the recovery, reclamation, and restoration of their 'lunatics', 'prisoners', 'women', and 'children'. Ordinances to make these effective were promulgated in India and Pakistan in January 1948 and May 1948 respectively, followed up by periodical conferences between the two countries to facilitate the recovery and restoration of women who had been abducted in the course of partition. The Abducted Persons (Recovery and Restoration) Act was passed by the Constituent Assembly of India on 15 December 1949 and remained in force for eight years until 1957. A similar act was passed in Pakistan to facilitate the recovery and restoration to India of Hindu and Sikh women and children who had been abducted in the course of partition.

An 'abducted person' under the Abducted Persons (Recovery and Restoration) Act in India meant:

... a male child under the age of sixteen years or a female of whatever age who is, or immediately before the first day of March, 1947, was a Muslim and who, on or after that day and before the first day of January 1949, has become separated from his or her family and is found to be living with or under the control of any other individual or family, and in the latter case includes a child born to any such female after the said date.

Muslim women recovered as abducted women in India under this law were taken into custody and placed in detention camps for restoration to their families in Pakistan. They could not lay any claims to Indian citizenship and the law did not allow judicial scrutiny of the recovery and restoration process. Feminist writings have interrogated the recovery of abducted women, the legal regime that facilitated it, and notions of state and national sovereignty that stressed its indispensability. While the two governments had resolved to restore women to their homes, and thereby refused to recognize the 'forced marriages' that had taken place in the course of this period, studies have shown that the long period that lapsed between abduction and recovery, and in some cases where women were left behind in the protection of a known family, made the process of recovery more complex than law made it out to be. Studies have shown that some among the recovered abducted women refused to return to their families, and expressed the wish to stay on with their abductors (Butalia 2006: 144). In cases where there were children 'born out of "wrong" sexual unions' (Das 1995: 73), the question of legal recognition and custody became contentious. In *State of Punjab* v. *Ajaib Singh*[1] (1952), for example, the questions that occupied the attention of the judges and assumed crucial importance in the judgement, concerned the fundamental rights of citizens against unlawful arrest, and the unconstitutionality, therefore, of the Abducted Persons (Recovery and Restoration) Act. This was perhaps the critical reason why the case could break free from the legal foreclosure prescribed by the act, allowing the case to be argued before both the high court and the Supreme Court. The details of the case as brought out in the Supreme Court judgement were as follows. In February 1951, Major Babu Singh reported that Ajaib Singh was holding three abducted persons. Subsequently, the recovery police of Ferozepore visited Ajaib Singh's house in village Shersingwala, took a 12-year-old girl Musammat Sardaran into custody, and delivered her to the custody of the officer

[1] AIR 10 1953 SCR 254.

in charge of the Muslim Transit Camp in Ferozepore. Musammat Sardaran was later transferred to the Recovered Muslim Women's Camp in Jalandhar. Nibar Dutt Sharma, a Sub-Inspector of Police, enquired into the facts of the case and concluded that Musammat Sardaran had indeed been abducted by Ajaib Singh. On 5 November 1951, Ajaib Singh filed a habeas corpus petition and obtained an interim order from the Punjab High Court that Musammat Sardaran should not be removed from Jalandhar until the disposal of the petition. The case was then enquired into by two Deputy Superintendents of Police (DSPs), one from India and the other from Pakistan. After considering the sub-inspector's report and the statements made before them by the girl, her mother who appeared before them while the enquiry was in progress, and Ghulam Rasul, the girl's uncle, the DSPs came to the conclusion that Musammat Sardaran was an abducted person as defined in the act and recommended that she should be sent to Pakistan 'for restoration to her next of kin'. The restoration was, however, to be kept in abeyance until the high court reached a decision in Ajaib Singh's appeal. On 26 November 1951, the habeas corpus petition came up for hearing before

Justices Bhandari and Khosla of Punjab High Court, who referred it to the full bench of the Supreme Court.

The grounds on which competing claims were made by Ajaib Singh and the government of Punjab over the 'custody' of Musammat Sardaran inadvertently drew the Supreme Court and the Government of India, into contest. As the custodian of the fundamental rights of citizens enumerated in the Constitution of India, which had come into force recently, the Supreme Court was pitted against the 'competence' of the government to legislate and take decisions on matters which inevitably had ramifications for citizens' rights. On the other hand, the legal regulation of recovery and restoration of abducted women was being construed as a serious matter concerning the nation, which notionally (and in practice) predated the constitution. Indeed, this inviolability of the context was recognized by the judges in their recreation of the trajectory of events, which had led to the enactment of the Abducted Persons Act. The judgement delivered in November 1952 by the Supreme Court bench comprising Justices Sudhi Ranjan Das, M. Patanjali Sastri, B.K. Mukherjea, Vivian Bose, and N.H. Bhagwati mentioned the 'heartrending' tales of partition, and the worth of the act as

18

a 'beneficial document'. Importantly, however, rather than pitching their final arguments within a framework that reinforced the logic of the nation, the judges invoked the logic of legal-constitutionalism, reclaiming the space for civic citizenship which the extraordinary measures under the act precluded.

Examining the consistency of the act with the constitution, both the High Court of Punjab and the Supreme Court concluded that the recovery procedures were subject to the jurisdiction of the high courts. In addition, recovered persons were entitled to the protection provided by Article 22 of the constitution, which lay down procedures pertaining specifically to arrests, detention, and loss of personal liberty. More significant, however, was the deliberation within the judgement on whether marking out Muslims as a specially defined class for the purpose of the act amounted to religious discrimination, and whether a case could be made against the state of having discriminated against abducted persons who happen to be citizens of India, on the ground of religion alone. Interestingly, however, nowhere does the judgement bring into consideration, and reveal thereby, whether Musammat Sardaran had exhibited any personal choice in the contest over her custody. Musammat Sardaran is an absent referent in the judgement, so that the specific circumstances of her case are submerged in the general pattern of abductions following partition, and it is the act and the constitution that are eventually foregrounded. Thus Musammat Sardaran is set at liberty not because the judges believed that *she* wanted it, but because they found procedural flaws in the act, ventured to bring it within the jurisdiction of the high court, and set out to restore the fundamental rights of Musammat Sardaran, on the assumption that despite her recovery, it could not be said conclusively that she was not a citizen of India. Significantly, while detained under the act, Sardaran was under a state of suspended citizenship, with no personal liberties. The Supreme Court restored Sardaran to citizenship, ironically by turning her detention into an arrest, and ordered her release on bail. Thus, her transition from a detainee non-citizen divested of any rights under the act to a citizen involved a subtle process of criminalization.

It is significant that relocation itself was determined by the different ways in which the western and eastern borders of India were construed. While the legal freezing of the western border was almost instantaneous, and the process of sifting outsiders (Muslim women in Hindu homes in India) and identifying and recovering the dislocated insiders (Hindu/Sikh women in Pakistan), was carried out as a task essential for the consummation of the nationalist project, the eastern border remained more or less fluid. Thus, if the congealing of the western border and legal resolution of the citizenship question threw up 'awkward' citizens in the form of women and children who needed to be restored to the nation, the eastern border continued to see the flow of people beyond the constitutional deadline of 19 July 1948, leading to a situation where their presence became 'illegal'. As a result, there can be seen a continuing ambivalence in the articulation of citizenship along the eastern border—which has resonated in the amendments to the citizenship act in 1986 and 2003/2005 and the Supreme Court decisions in later years in cases relating to migration across the eastern borders into India.

It is worth repeating here that the amendment to the citizenship act in 1986 pertained to the question of citizenship in Assam and the identification and sifting out of illegal migrants in the state. The inflow of people from the adjoining areas of East Bengal into Assam sustained from the early decades of the twentieth century as Muslim peasants from Mymensingh, Pabna, Bogra, and Rangapur settled in Goalpara, and moved on to Nowgong, Kamrup (then Barpeta district), and Darrang, and later to North Lakhimpur district, occupying most of the wasteland. After Independence, the influx into Assam of what now became an East Pakistani population continued across the still fluid border. As pointed out earlier, unlike the exchange and flow of population on the western border, where the constitutional deadline for migrants from Pakistan to claim citizenship in India was treated as final, the eastern border remained permeable for some time.

In her study of 'refugee women' drawn from the recollections of women and families coming out of the partition of Bengal, Gargi Chakravartty (2005) shows how despite the violence, rape, abduction, and killings that engulfed areas like Noakhali and Tippera (October 1946) and the massacre of Hindus and abduction of women in Kolkata (16–19 August 1946), which instilled a deep insecurity among Hindus in East Bengal, they thought that partition, like Bengal's earlier partition in 1905, would be a temporary phenomenon, and did not leave their ancestral homes to

22

migrate permanently to India. Yet, the loss of status of middle-class Hindus, continuing insecurity, discrimination, and repression by the state, and finally the riots in 1950, compelled their steady migration to India. From February to April 1950, streams of refugees (10,000 refugees every day) arrived in West Bengal and Tripura. Sealdah station in particular was flooded with 'dispossessed and unattached women' sent by their men to seek security in India (Chakravartty 2005: 7–47).

Following the violence of partition and migration of (Hindu) minorities from East Pakistan, the Nehru–Liaquat pact prescribed that refugees returning home to East Pakistan by 31 December 1950 would be entitled to get back their property, effectively pushing the date beyond the constitutional deadline of 19 July 1948. In the 1971 Bangladesh war, several lakhs of Hindu and Muslim refugees fled to Assam. In a Joint Declaration on 8 February 1972, the Prime Ministers of the two countries assured 'the continuance of all possible assistance to the Government of Bangladesh in the unprecedented task of resettling the refugees and displaced persons in Bangladesh' (Baruah 1999: 119). While not all refugees returned to Bangladesh, more migrants continued to cross the border into Assam and other parts of India in search of livelihood. Within Assam, the presence of large numbers of 'foreigners' instilled a sense of unease at the change in demography, language, and access to resources, primarily land, and employment, around which a powerful popular movement erupted.

Throughout the 1980s, the Assam movement lay claim to a distinctive Assamese identity and based on this, a differentiated citizenship. Grounded in the principle of 'different yet equal', 'difference' was articulated in the initial years of the movement in terms of the linguistic/cultural identity of the Assamese, and later with the United Liberation Front of Assam (ULFA) taking over the struggle, in terms of unequal development and discrimination spelling from the differential terms of inclusion of Assam into the national-political space. If the former was grounded in issues of an Assamese ethnic identity, the latter chose to prioritize issues of development and access to resources. At the root of both, however, was the crisis in citizenship in Assam. The central government sought to pacify the movement through a series of coercive policies, including a range of extraordinary laws to tame the movement, repression by the state machinery, and a series of forced elections. Yet the model of citizenship that the Assam movement seemed to invoke replicated the universal form that it was seeking to roll back in its own relationship with the Indian state. These contradictions played out in the articulation of citizenship at the national and state levels and within the state between the 'ethnic' Assamese and the Bodos, the Assamese and the Bengalis, the Assamese and the tribals, and so on. Significantly, as the discussion in the next section will bear out, while development concerns were addressed in the Assam Accord of 1985 between the leaders of the movement and the Indian government, the amendment to the Citizenship Act following the Accord reinforced hierarchical citizenship in Assam by identifying the Bangladeshi (illegal) migrant as the absolute other.

The 'Politics of Place Making' and 'Suspect Citizens'

Citizenship is a federal subject and Article 11 of the constitution gives the Indian Parliament paramount power to regulate and determine it. As mentioned earlier, Part II of the constitution gave the Parliament overriding powers 'to regulate the right of citizenship by law' and make provisions for its acquisition and termination, and all other matters pertaining to citizenship subsequent to the commencement of the constitution (Article 11). The Parliament enacted the Citizenship Act of 1955 with elaborate provisions specifying how citizenship could be acquired by birth, descent, registration, naturalization, or through incorporation of territory. While the constitution had provided for the framework within which the rights of citizenship of persons migrating between India and Pakistan could be determined (Articles 6 and 7), the migrant made an appearance in the Citizenship Act through an amendment in 1986. The figure of the migrant was in fact central to the Citizenship (Amendment) Act of 1986. Unlike its incorporation in the Constitution of India, in which migration was one of the conditions of passage into citizenship, in 1986 migration was associated with illegality and disqualification from citizenship.

Coming after a long-drawn struggle in Assam against the presence of 'foreigners' and 'illegal aliens', the amendment introduced a sixth category of citizenship, which was to apply exclusively to Assam. The amendment may be construed as a moment of encompassment, opening up within the framework of citizenship a space for the articulation of difference by incorporating the Assamese exception in the citizenship law. Yet, closure as a differential experience of citizenship followed closely. The political contexts and discursive practices of citizenship preceding the amendment and those that followed it, show that citizenship was embedded inextricably in what Sanjib Baruah (2005) describes most appropriately as the politics of 'nationalisation of space' and 'place making' in which the 'national space' emerges as ordered, bounded, and differentiated. This politics included the use of technologies of control and repression against the people of the region struggling against the hegemony of the Indian state for the recognition of regional ethno-spaces. Significantly, the negotiations between the movement and the central government over the 'illegal migrant' and legal measures to identify and sift him/her out, also became occasions when the central government reclaimed and affirmed its authority to define the terms of legal membership of the Indian nation state.

The political and legal manoeuvrings that unfolded in the 1980s, through the Assam Accord (1985) and the amendment to the Citizenship Act in 1986, show that the central government projected the issue of 'foreigners' and 'illegal migrants' in Assam as an *Assamese* anxiety, not involving national concerns. Indeed, in an attempt to delegitimize the movement as subversive of the nation state, the government sought to smother it through constitutional means, namely, elections, and repressive measures like the National Security Act, 1980, the Disturbed Areas Act, 1955, and Armed Forces Special Powers Act, 1958. The Assam Accord between the leaders of the Assam movement and the central government was couched in a language that projected the government's alertness to the 'genuine apprehensions of the people of Assam'. Holding out the promise of 'constitutional, legislative and administrative safeguards ... to protect, preserve and promote the cultural, social, linguistic identity and heritage of the Assamese people', the accord ultimately affirmed the central government's constitutional role as the final arbiter in matters concerning citizenship. Although it put in place exceptional provisions of citizenship in Assam, the continued application of the Illegal Migrants (Determination by Tribunal) Act of 1983 (henceforth IMDT Act) showed that even as it gave way to the demands of the Assam agitation on the 'foreigners' question, by sustaining the application of the IMDT Act, the central government retained exclusive authority over all matters concerning citizenship.

Before examining the various provisions of the IMDT Act and elaborating on why it became a festering issue in the resolution of the citizenship question in Assam, it is important to draw attention to the fact that the foreigners' issue became a significant political concern because of its implication for the electoral processes in Assam. While anxieties around the presence of foreigners and illegal migrants in Assam remained more or less subterranean in the years after Independence, a prolonged movement around the issue was set off by a by-election held in 1979 in Mangaldai Parliamentary constituency following the death of the sitting MP. The revision of the voter list for the by-election drew attention to the extraordinary rise in the number of voters, giving way to the suspicion that the increase was the result of enrolment of foreigners as voters. The All Assam Students' Union (AASU) organized a rally on 6 November 1979 at Guwahati demanding the immediate settlement of the foreigners' issue. Led by Prafulla Kumar Mahanta and

Bhrigu Kumar Phukan, the rally marked the begin-
ning of a prolonged struggle. The AASU, supported
by several regional parties and major literary associations of Assam, demanded the screening of the electoral rolls the Election Commission had prepared in
order to eliminate illegal migrants. The Chief Election
Commissioner, S.L. Shakdher, also commented on the
demographic changes in the state while referring to the
census records of 1971 to report the 'alarming situation' arising out of unprecedented inflation in electoral
rolls in Assam. The Election Commission cancelled the
election in 12 out of Assam's 14 Parliamentary seats
with the result that following the 1980 Parliamentary
elections Assam remained unrepresented or under-
represented in the Lok Sabha for almost the entire
duration of the Assam movement. In the meantime,
the state government remained unstable with short
periods of Congress(I) governments, interspersed with
President's rule. In March 1982, the state government
elected in 1978 was dissolved, and the state placed
once again under President's rule, which in turn neces-
sitated adherence to the constitutional requirement
of holding elections within a year of its imposition.
The election to the state government was eventually

held in February 1983 amidst unprecedented violence. Simultaneously, elections to the Legislative Assembly and 12 Parliamentary seats that remained vacant from the previous election were held. Significantly, concerns were raised that conditions in Assam were not conducive for polls and could deepen the existing divide. While the election commissioner held that if a legal alternative were available he would postpone the election, the central government persisted with the policy of snuffing out the movement in Assam 'politically' through the electoral process. The AASU and the All Assam Gana Sangram Parishad (AAGSP) decided to boycott what they considered to be an illegal election, since the issue of 'who was entitled to vote', which was at the crux of the movement, remained unresolved.

Elections were conducted under extraordinary circumstances as parts of Assam were declared 'disturbed areas', and several AASU and AAGSP activists were detained. The election process was steeped in unprecedented violence so much so that it earned the epithet of the 'bloody election'. The 1983 elections brought to power a Congress(I) government led by Hiteshwar Saikia. The IMDT Act passed in 1983 by the central government at a time when Assam continued to be largely unrepresented in the Parliament, put in place legal procedures that made it difficult to identify an 'illegal' migrant. While the act was to extend to the whole of India, its applicability to Assam was immediately notified, so that it took effect immediately in the state of Assam, coming into force on 15 October 1983.

There were significant differences between the Foreigners Act, 1946, which had been used to settle disputes on the identification of citizens in India, and the IMDT Act, 1983. The IMDT Act's stipulations regarding the identification of illegal migrants gave a central tribunal the final power of determination, thus making the identification more difficult. Whereas under the Foreigners Act, a person identified as a foreigner bore the burden of proving that she/he was not one, under the IMDT Act the burden of proof was shifted to the identifying authority. Under the IMDT Act, a foreigner (as defined under the Foreigners Act, 1946), who had entered India on or after 25 March 1971, and did not possess a valid passport or other travel documents, would be considered an illegal migrant. Under Section 5(1) of the IMDT Act, the central government was authorized to set up tribunals that could take up 'references' and 'applications'.

In response to a 'reference' from a person identified as a foreigner under the Foreigners Act, the tribunal gave the individual thirty days to furnish proof in his/her defence. On the other hand, an authority making an 'application' declaring someone a foreigner was asked to furnish a report with evidence substantiating its allegations. While anyone could petition the tribunal regarding a third person who was said to be an illegal migrant, the tribunal would not entertain such an application unless the person in relation to whom the application was made was residing within three kilometres from the place of residence of the petitioner. In addition, every application had to be accompanied by corroborating affidavits sworn by at least two other persons who also resided within the three-kilometre radius. Moreover, both the reference and the application could be made to the tribunal only within the particular territorial jurisdiction in which the alleged 'illegal migrant' resided. Thus, the procedures prescribed for the process of identification under the IMDT Act (unlike those under the Foreigners Act) were tedious and accounted for the low rates of identification of illegal migrants under the act. Not surprisingly, therefore, despite the Assam Accord of 1985, the

IMDT Act continued to generate rancour in Assam until 2005, when the Supreme Court scrapped it.

As mentioned before, the accord reached between the Rajiv Gandhi government and the leaders of the Assam movement on 15 August 1985 was a broad settlement on cultural and economic development concerns, which included the promise by the central government to ensure 'constitutional, legislative and administrative safeguards ... to protect, preserve and promote the cultural, social, linguistic identity and heritage of the Assamese people' and the 'all round economic development of Assam'. On the question of 'foreigners' in Assam, the accord evolved a *graded/differentiated* system, categorizing them on the basis of the date on which they had entered India. It legitimized the citizenship status of a large number of immigrants who had come before 1966. Those who had entered the state between January 1966 and 25 March 1971 were to be legitimized in phases, that is, they were to be disenfranchised for a period of ten years, while others who had come after March 1971, were to be deported as illegal aliens. It was also agreed that the state government formed after the elections of 1983 would resign, the state assembly would be dissolved, and fresh elections based on revised electoral rolls be held in December 1985. In November 1986, the Parliament enacted an amendment to India's citizenship law giving effect to the provisions of the accord.

The Citizenship Act, 1955 was accordingly amended in 1986, adding Article 6A, which made way for a sixth category of citizenship along with birth, descent, registration, naturalization, and by incorporation of foreign territory into India. The amended act laid down that (i) all persons of Indian origin who came to Assam before 1 January 1966 from a specified territory (meaning territories included in Bangladesh) and had been ordinarily resident in Assam would be considered citizens of India from the date unless they chose not to be; (ii) (a) persons of Indian origin from the specified territories who came on or after 1 January 1966 but before 25 March 1971 and had been resident in Assam since and (b) had been detected in accordance with the provisions of the Foreigners Act, 1946 and Foreigners (Tribunals) Orders, 1964 (c) upon registration, would be considered citizens of India, from the date of expiry of a period of ten years from the date of detection as a foreigner. In the interim period, they would enjoy all facilities including Indian passports, but would not have the right to vote. All other persons who entered the state after 25 March 1971, upon identification as illegal migrants under the IMDT Act, would be deported.

With the signing of the Assam Accord, we can see the confirmation of a hierarchized model of citizenship constituted by the 'universal we', the Assamese people, whose claims to citizenship was beyond any legal disputation. The universal 'we' was superimposed on residual citizens, whose citizenship was rendered ambivalent by their linguistic identity or their religion. It was sought to resolve this ambivalence legally by conferring deferred citizenship onto some (those who arrived between 1966 and 25 March 1971), through the determination of their legality by the Foreigners Act. The rest, that is, those who arrived in India after 25 March 1971, were aliens. The illegality of their presence was to be confirmed by the IMDT Act, for subsequent deportation from India. In actual practice, however, since both the Foreigners Act and the IMDT Act were to apply simultaneously, and the two prescribed different modes of determining citizenship, in a context of the continuing influx of immigrants from Bangladesh the residual citizens continue to occupy a zone of perpetually indeterminate citizenship and suspect legality. On the other hand, as far as the mode of identification of 'illegal migrant' or 'foreigner' was concerned, the IMDT Act was more 'protective' of the interests of the immigrant, since it shifted the responsibility of proving legal residence from the person 'identified' to a 'prescribed authority', and demanded a locus standi from the applicant identifying the 'illegal migrant'. Thus, even as the 1986 amendment introduced an exception into the legal-formal frameworks of citizenship in India, expressing a legal recognition of the special circumstances that existed in Assam, there were contradictory layers in this exception.

The IMDT Act was scrapped in 2005 by the Supreme Court removing thereby, what was largely seen in Assam as an anomalous and unfair exception. In its judgement, delivered on 12 August 2005, almost five years after a petition seeking its repeal was made by Sarbananda Sonowal, a former President of AASU, former MLA for the Assam Gana Parishad, and an MP, a three-judge Supreme Court bench declared the IMDT Act unconstitutional. The grounds on which the Supreme Court declared the act unconstitutional were specifically questions of legal procedure, but the

general principles articulated in the process have ramifications for the way in which the terms of citizenship get defined and interpreted. While declaring the
IMDT Act unconstitutional, the court described
migration not merely as illegal entry into a foreign
territory, but as *an act of aggression*. Arguing within a
bounded notion of citizenship, the Supreme Court
regarded the buttressing of national territorial boundaries and the protection of its population, an integral
component of state sovereignty. Moreover, the judges
marked out the migrant not only for being an alien,
but also for being a Muslim. The illegal Muslim
migrant is inevitably associated with Islamic funda-
mentalism, and construed as a threat to national security. Manifesting the political–ideological contexts of
the period, the judgement discussed the demographic
shifts in Assam following the influx of illegal migrants
from Bangladesh not in terms of changes in the linguistic profile of the state, but in terms of its religious
profile, emphasizing the increase in the Muslim population, and the threat it posed not just to Assam but to
all of India.

The judgement may be read as embedded in the
dominant frameworks of nationalism which cast a web

of suspicion around all Bengali-speaking Muslims in Assam and the rest of the country. It may also be seen as a consummation of institutional and state practices that had been unfolding throughout the 1990s and manifested in the vicious cycle of dispossession, dislocation, disenfranchisement, and violence against Muslim residents of Delhi slums on the assumption that they were illegal migrants. The Supreme Court judgement scrapping the IMDT Act reflected a trend towards the entrenchment of a notion of citizenship marked by blood ties and cultural ascriptions which had almost imperceptibly crept into the Citizenship Act with the amendment in 1986, and may be seen as consummating with the Citizenship (Amendment) Act of 2003.

The Deception of Deterritoriality

The Citizenship (Amendment) Act of 2003 introduced a version of dual/transnational citizenship for Persons of Indian Origin (PIOs) by inserting the category of OCI. Under the amended act, an OCI was a person of Indian origin and citizen of another country, or was a citizen of India immediately before becoming a citizen of another country, and got registered as an OCI. The OCI may be seen as embodying several competing and dissonant strands. An influential trend sees the OCI as part of a global tendency towards transnationalism. Since the late 1980s, there has been an upsurge in writings on citizenship. Most of the writing professes that conditions specifically in the late twentieth century—the globalization of economy, the unprecedented scale of transnational movement of workers and refugees, the cataclysmic effects of technological and economic expansion and flow of information, and so forth—have diminished the centrality of the nation state as the primary unit of political membership and identity. The idea of a singular territorially inscribed citizenship, they argue, is no longer relevant in a connected world. Seen in this way, the OCI may be seen as an encompassing moment since it transcends the limits imposed on citizenship by territorially bounded membership of nation states.

Alongside these claims of transnationality and globality of citizenship, however, there may be identified a dissonant note expressed in the anxiety over a 'crisis' in citizenship. The lament of crisis is evident not only in writings on global citizenship, but also in the state practices, which perhaps more vehemently than ever before, have striven to reinforce nation state boundaries, restricting the inflow of foreigners, immigrants, and refugees. Citizenship itself gets defined in exclusionary terms and emerges as the bastion on which the nation state asserts its sovereignty and fortifies itself against the 'hordes of starving people'. More significant, however, is the manner in which transnational citizenship generates unease and apprehensions in specific national locations. Seen as precipitating a 'duality' in citizenship in the 'host' country, transnational citizenship generates anxieties around the weakening bonds of community identity and social solidarity that make for robust citizenship. More significant, however, is the way in which what appears to be an 'opening up' of narrowly defined territorial citizenship through an introduction of extraterritoriality, is the simultaneous 'closing of ranks' with citizenship by birth giving way to citizenship by descent.

Ironically, while a dominant suggestion seems to be that the OCI embodies deterritorialized citizenship, the claimed deterritorialization is both ironic and deceptive. While the amendments bringing in the category of the OCI indeed lifted the legal–constitutional closure from Indian citizenship which the assumption of the citizenship of a foreign country brought in its wake, the foreclosure for those PIOs who had made the choice of opting out of Indian citizenship in preference for Pakistani citizenship continued. At the same time, the amendment also manifests a trend followed by several countries, especially those which had integrated in some significant way in the hierarchized world economy and had assumed the position of 'fast developing economies', to reach out to their diaspora in various ways, not the least, opening up for them avenues of investment in their countries of origin.

The report of the High Level/Powered Committee on the Indian Diaspora, headed by L.M. Singhvi, which was set up in August 2000 to suggest the framework for facilitating the association of the Indian diaspora with India in 'a mutually beneficial relationship', embodied all these strands. Emphasizing the ubiquitous presence of the Indian diaspora, the Committee inverted the logic of imperialism, when it declared: 'The Indian diaspora spans the globe and stretches across all the continents. It is so widespread that the sun never sets on it' (Ministry of External Affairs 2002: 2). Even as the report highlighted the vast numbers of the diaspora ('estimated to be about 20 million'), their diversity, and spread across the globe, it carefully underscored their common identity: 'They live in different countries, speak different languages, and are engaged in different pursuits. What gives them their common identity is their Indian origin, their cultural heritage, their deep attachment to India' (Ministry of External Affairs 2002: 2).

It is significant that the Singhvi Committee Report projected overseas citizenship as a 'new' *setubandhan* (building ties/bridges) in our time. While the allusion to the 'original' setubandhan undertaken by Rama to rescue Sita is apparent, given the contexts of the emotional bonds and cultural linkages that the report emphasizes, the 'new' setubandhan connotes the recovery and cementing of the natural/blood/ethnic bonds. Setubandhan, the report, never fails to reiterate, brings about the affirmation of an existing natural bond, which the acquisition of citizenship of a foreign country and the subsequent renunciation of Indian citizenship fails to excise. It, therefore, disproportionately emphasizes the 'emotional needs' of the diaspora, as the primary justification for dual citizenship, dispelling the notion that the OCI may also have a material basis:

'We do not wish to advocate dual nationality only for diaspora remittances, important though they are to India's development.... The principal rationales of the demand of the Diaspora for dual citizenship, however, is sentimental and psychological, a consideration which commends itself to the Committee in the same measure as do social, economic and political factors' (Ministry of External Affairs 2002).

That the diaspora 'yearns' for close emotional ties and 'needs' them, is a constant refrain, '[They] have taken up the nationality of the country of their domicile but look upon their passports with nostalgia.' That such unhappiness and sadness is a manifestation of natural and inextricable ties, deeply embedded in a 'continuous civilization' is stressed repeatedly. Under the heading 'Culture', the report notes the 'deep commitment to their cultural identity [that] has manifested in the component of the Indian diaspora, the members of the diaspora identify with Indians, equally the inheritors of the traditions of a continuous civilization'. The emphasis on continuity paves the ground for bringing the second generation of overseas Indians, that is, those who were not born in India, within the purview of overseas citizenship, for:

44

... perpetuating and cementing the links of the younger generation of the diaspora with India as they will be keen to keep in touch with their elders in India as well as relate to their roots.... The members of the Indian diaspora are naturally keen to pass on their value systems, which have been a reason of their success to coming generations, and they would welcome our country's support in this endeavour. India should also initiate measures to ensure that the diaspora's pride and faith in it are strengthened, which would inter-alia revitalise its internal development. (Ministry of External Affairs 2002: 511)

After the tribute to the expanse and cultural cohesion of the diaspora, it perhaps seems ironic that the Singhvi Committee Report, in the first instance, limited the universe of OCI to specific countries of North America, Europe, and Australasia, compelling the observation by Fatima Meer, a member of the African National Congress, that the OCI as articulated by the Singhvi Committee was nothing more than 'dollar and pound citizenship' (Reddy 2003). That monetary considerations were never absent, even though care was taken not to make them appear primary, is evident from the fact that among the suggestions put forward

45

by the Singhvi Committee was the setting up of Special Economic Zones (SEZs), exclusively for projects to be undertaken by OCIs, PIOs, and NRIs.

The debate on the Citizenship Amendment Bill 2003 under the Bharatiya Janata Party (BJP)-led National Democratic Alliance (NDA) government saw a reiteration of this emotional link and desire for closer ties. While moving the motion in the Rajya Sabha after receiving the report on the Bill by the Parliamentary Standing Committee, L.K. Advani, then Minister of Home Affairs, justified the Bill not only on the grounds of the warm ties the diaspora 'continue to have with India and Indian culture', but as a measure to bring the 'diaspora *closer to themselves and to India*'.[2] He recommended observing 9 and 10 December as Pravasi Bharatiya Divas, the first such event having been organized in 2003. Incidentally, the symbolic value of 9 December, the date of Gandhi's 'return' to India from South Africa was also commented upon. The speech of Manmohan Singh, then leader of the Opposition in the Rajya Sabha, likewise alluded to emotional ties while also referring to the diaspora as 'a great national

[2] Debates in the Rajya Sabha, 19 December 2003.

reservoir', whose 'knowledge, wealth, experience and expertise' could 'be tapped for the benefit of our country'.[3] The Singhvi Committee recommended that 'dual citizenship' should be permitted within the rubric of the Citizenship Act, 1955, suggesting also that Sections 9, 10, and 12 of the act should be suitably amended.

A bill to amend the existing Citizenship Act was introduced in the Rajya Sabha on 9 May 2003 and subsequently referred to the Standing Committee chaired by Pranab Mukherjee[4] for examination and report. The Standing Committee's report (12 December 2003) endorsed the amendment to the Citizenship Act, 1955 to make provisions pertaining to the grant of Overseas Citizenship of India. Significantly, alongside, it also recommended the introduction of a scheme for compulsory registration of every citizen of India accompanied by the issue of national identity cards, making acquisition of Indian citizenship by registration and naturalization more stringent, preventing

[3] Debates in the Rajya Sabha, 19 December 2003.

[4] Report of the Standing Committee, One Hundred and Seventh Report on the Citizenship Amendment Bill, 2003, Government of India, Delhi.

illegal migrants from becoming eligible for Indian citizenship, and simplifying the procedure to facilitate the reacquisition of Indian citizenship by persons of full age who are children of Indian citizens and former citizens of independent India. As far as the specific changes in the Citizenship Act were concerned, the Singhvi Committee recommended that dual citizenship should be permitted within the rubric of the Citizenship Act, 1955, suggesting that Sections 9, 10, and 12 of the Citizenship Act, 1955, which dealt with conditions of termination of citizenship and principles of reciprocity in matters of conferment of rights to citizens of Commonwealth countries, should be amended.

The Citizenship Amendment Act, 2003 made several amendments to existing sections and inserted Sections 7A, 7B, 7C, and 7D titled 'Overseas Citizens of India' that dealt with the definition and registration of overseas citizens, conferred specific rights to them while also identifying the rights that did not belong to them, and the conditions under which the registration could be cancelled. While registration of an overseas Indian citizen was made subject to conditions and restrictions including the condition of reciprocity, the rights from which such a citizen was especially barred were the rights to equality of opportunity in matters of public employment, contesting elections for the post of President or Vice President of India, appointment as judge of the Supreme Court and high courts, voting rights, contesting elections to the Legislative Assembly or Legislative Council and appointment to public services and posts in connection with the affairs of the union or any state.

The act provided that the central government could, on application, register any PIO as an OCI if that person was a citizen of another country and one which allowed dual citizenship. Such a PIO could become an OCI if she/he (a) was a citizen of India on 26 January 1950 or at any time thereafter; (b) was eligible to become a citizen of India on 26 January 1950; (c) belonged to a territory that became part of India after the 15th day of August, 1947; (d) was the child or grandchild of a person described above; and (e) had never been a citizen of Pakistan or Bangladesh. The act authorized Indian Missions to grant applications for overseas citizenship of India within fifteen days in cases where there was no involvement in serious offences like drug trafficking, moral turpitude, terrorist activities, or anything leading to imprisonment of more than a year. Overseas Indian Citizenship did not entitle people who had acquired, or were planning to acquire, foreign nationality, to retain their Indian passports. The law continued to require that Indian citizens who took foreign nationality must immediately surrender their Indian passports. Those who were eligible could then apply for registration as OCI. It is worth reiterating that while defining eligibility and what constituted Indian origin to qualify for overseas citizenship of India, the act retained the contexts of partition and the excision of those who had become Pakistani citizens (including citizens of Bangladesh).

An amendment to the Citizenship Act in June 2005, allowed the scheme to cover PIOs in other countries, who had emigrated after 1950 and were living in any country other than Bangladesh and Pakistan. The extension of the status to countries other than those identified in 2003, is significant since, in 2005 the overseas Indians sent remittances to India at an estimated 21.7 billion dollars, more than what China (21.3 billion) and Mexico (18 billion) received. More than half such remittances were by West Asia-based Indians, with Kerala being the single largest beneficiary.

In their statements of objects and reasons, the Citizenship (Amendment) Act, 2003 claimed to be providing 'dual citizenship' to persons of Indian origin. It must be remembered, however, that the amendment actually put in place a variant of transnational citizenship, which fell short of being 'dual' citizenship, since it did not provide the overseas Indian with an Indian passport. Under Section 9 of the Citizenship Act of 1955, if a person 'voluntarily' acquires the citizenship of another country, her/his Indian citizenship is terminated. A PIO who has acquired the citizenship of another country is no longer an Indian citizen and cannot, therefore, hold an Indian passport. The status of an OCI does not entitle people who have acquired, or are planning to acquire, foreign nationality, to retain or reacquire their Indian passports, which were surrendered when they acquired the citizenship of another country. The OCI was allowed under the amended act, the 'overseas Indian citizen card', which spelt some privileges for the cardholder, including a lifelong visa. Dual citizenship as practiced in countries which permit it would also imply that a citizen of another country, who has acquired Indian citizenship, could simultaneously hold the passport of her/his country of origin, and continue being a citizen of both the countries. The Indian laws pertaining to citizenship by naturalization specifically lay down renunciation of any other citizenship, if an application for Indian citizenship has been accepted by the Indian government.

Ten years after the OCI was expanded, an Ordinance was promulgated in January 2015 by the BJP-led NDA government erasing the difference between the PIO and OCI schemes. Among the benefits that the OCIs enjoy is a lifelong visa for visiting India, and exemption from registration with the local police. They are explicitly denied the right to vote. A PIO on the other hand, following a notification by the Government of India in 2002, is a person who was at any time an Indian citizen, or if she or her parents or grandparents or great-grandparents were born in or were permanently resident in India as defined in the Government of India Act, 1935 and other territories that became part of India thereafter provided neither was at any time a citizen of Afghanistan, Bhutan, China, Nepal, Pakistan, and Sri Lanka. Unlike the OCI, the PIO cardholder does not have a lifelong visa, and is exempt from the requirement of registration only if the stay in a single visit did not exceed 180 days.

Largely seen as the fulfilment of a promise made by Prime Minister Narendra Modi in September 2014 to a mammoth gathering of the Indian diaspora in Madison Square in New York City, steps in this direction had already been taken by the UPA government in January 2010 when the merger of the two schemes was proposed in the first meeting of the Prime Minister's Global Advisory Council of Overseas Indians. Inaugurating the 9th Pravasi Bharatiya Divas in January 2011, then Prime Minister Manmohan Singh had expressed the intention of his government to make a single scheme operational. On 8 and 9 January 2015, the pravasi Indians gathered in Gandhinagar in Gujarat for the annual Pravasi Bharatiya Divas, and also to commemorate 100 years of Gandhi's return to India. The 2015 Ordinance was timed to coincide with these celebrations, and yet again became a symbolic elaboration of the setubandhan recommended by the High Powered Committee on the Indian Diaspora. Replaced by a law in March 2015, the 2015 amendment act introduced yet another nomenclature replacing the OCI—the Overseas Citizen of India Cardholder. Apart from those who were eligible to become OCIs in the earlier amendment of 2005, the 2015 amendment made it possible for PIOs, minor children of Indian citizens living abroad, and spouses of foreign origin married to overseas citizens of India or Indian citizens living abroad, to become OCI cardholders.

In 2003, while announcing the recommendations of the Singhvi Committee and the proposed introduction of a new category of the OCI in the Citizenship Act, the then Prime Minister Atal Behari Vajpayee had declared: 'We are in favour of dual citizenship but not dual loyalty…. Indians settled abroad should also have loyalty to those countries'. Doing away with the requirement of an oath of allegiance for those registering as OCIs, the Parliamentary Standing Committee agreed that allegiance to the constitution could not be divided and such a requirement would interfere with the primary citizenship of the OCIs. The arguments by both Vajpayee and the Standing Committee capture the anxieties that are invoked by transnational, dual, or multiple citizenships.

The invocation of a state of primary belonging and membership based on 'blood', and the possibility of seeing this membership independent of patriotism and loyalty to the constitution which alludes to the civic elements of citizenship, has significant implications.

It allows for envisioning a benign, non-threatening condition of dual citizenship and transnational memberships, where a citizen can inhabit two worlds simultaneously, without causing any friction in the terms of membership demanded by each. Of these, the natural and constitutive world of the country of origin, and the idea of the home country, is carried to the new land. The assumption is that this constitutive world can exist autonomously, juxtaposed onto the new world of 'primary residence and work'. On the other hand, the impossibility of the compartmentalization of dual citizenship into non-abrasive and friction-free worlds of affective and effective belonging has precipitated a 'crisis in citizenship'. Significantly, the 'crisis' in citizenship seen as emerging from 'duality' of belonging and the subsequent weakening of bonds of solidarity and allegiance to the host/adopted countries of work, has been addressed through amendments in citizenship laws in most countries, which quite like those in India, follow a trend towards congealing of ethnic bonds for the promotion of solid citizenship.

The changes in the citizenship law in India capture the ferment in citizenship, which has become more accentuated in recent years, deepening the fault lines in the debates on the core features of citizenship. The constitutional provisions had opened up the closures generated by the drawing of territorial boundaries of the nation state in 1947, by attributing legibility to certain kinds of movements of people across borders that had taken place in the intervening period. The Citizenship Act of 1955 similarly held out the promise of legibility to those who occupied the space of liminal and indeterminate citizenship between 1950 and 1955. With the citizenship law yet to be enacted, people were travelling across borders on a variety of travel documents and permits. When the Citizenship Act came into force, the cross-border movements came to be imputed with ascriptions of legality and illegality. While the element of choice and voluntariness presented themselves as a legal possibility, there were tensions in the way in which choice was determined, seen especially in the finality with which the excision from citizenship was laid down in the constitution for those who had migrated to Pakistan after 1 March 1947, unless they had returned to India under a permit for resettlement or permanent residence, in which case they were considered to have migrated to India after 19 July 1948 and registered as citizens of India.

The cartographic anxieties of the past have assumed new forms, as the modes of making citizens legible has made the transition from documentary identification regimes to biometric mapping, to produce digital citizens. It needs to be emphasized that the preparation of a National Population Register (NPR), was provided for by the Citizenship Amendment Act, 2003 (through the insertion of Section 14 A, with effect from December 2004) and the Registration of Citizens and the issue of National Identity Cards Rules of 2003. The new insertion made the registration of all citizens of India, the issue of national identity cards, the maintenance of a national population register, and the establishment of a national registration authority by the central government, compulsory. At the basis of these practices is the concern around effective ways of sifting out illegal aliens, while securing your own citizens.

2

'We the People'

Citizenship in the Indian Constitution

The astonished gora made several efforts to save him-
self from the heavy blows raining down on him, but
when he noticed that his assailant was in a rage border-
ing on madness, and flames were shooting forth from
his eyes, he began to scream. His screams only made
Ustad Mango work his arms faster. He was thrashing
the gora to his heart's content while shouting, 'The
same cockiness even on 1st April! Well, sonny boy, it
is our Raj now.'

... Foaming at the mouth, with his smiling eyes he
was looking at the astonished crowd and saying in a
breathless voice, 'Those days are gone friends, when
they ruled the roost. There is a new constitution now,
fellows, a new constitution. ' (Manto 2008: 215)

The extract is from a short story '*Naya Kanoon*' (literally, the new law) written by Saadat Hasan Manto in the 1930s. Translated and published later with the title 'The New Constitution', the story narrated the bewitchment of Ustad Mango, the *tongawala*, with the idea of freedom. Mango was illiterate but was considered an Ustad by the fellow tongawalas of his adda because he was a man of wisdom and was versatile with a range of matters concerning the world. The story is about Mango's allurement with the idea of the new constitution, which held out the promise of delivering him from the indignity and humiliation he suffered on a daily basis from the inebriated British soldiers residing in the cantonment. For Mango, the promise of freedom remains unfulfilled, however, and indeed, it ends in disenchantment. The day the 'new law' was to come into force, Mango wakes up in the morning a new man. Steeped with the confidence of having finally become his own master, he consciously plies his tonga through the street to the place where his tormentor—the British soldier—was likely to be waiting for his tonga. To the utmost surprise of the soldier, Mango starts hitting and kicking him, venting the anger that had remained submerged all these years, and the anguish at having had to remain subservient and passive when he could have smashed the man to bits. Through this brief moment of violent outburst, Mango lives a cathartic euphoria of being a free man under the new constitution. Soon, however, the police arrives, picks him up, and puts him in a lock-up, stifling his chant of freedom with the reprimand: 'New constitution, new constitution! What rubbish are you talking? It's the same old constitution.'

'The New Constitution' was a story written with reference to the Government of India Act of 1935, which is an important signpost in the transition to constitutional democracy in India. In the history of constitutionalism in India, the 1935 Act has largely been seen as having provided the template for the Constitution of independent India. Manto's story conveys the significance of the new law for being the harbinger of hope, which lay in the promise of self-rule. Mango's exhilaration at having become a citizen, unconstrained by the rule of the outsider, turns into despair as old forms of domination continue. His estrangement from citizenship persists, and he remains a stranger in his own home. Mango's bewitchment and subsequent disenchantment with the new constitution spring from its failure to transform him into a sovereign political subject. His disappointment is indicative of the powerful affective appeal of the individual and collective transition to the camaraderie of equal citizenship, a promise that lies at the heart of the constitutive moment of transformative constitutionalism.

Transformative constitutionalism, argues Upendra Baxi (2013) is characteristic of constitution making practices in societies making the transition to democracy from colonial and authoritarian rule. An integral feature of postcolonial constitutionalism is a conscious and meticulous sequestering from an oppressive past. The national liberation struggle in India invoked the idea of a shared cultural past and traced a distinctive identity for the Indian nation. The inauguration of the Republican Constitution, however, embodied the momentous present, from where a vision of a future, different from the past, could be realized. This future had to rid itself of all residues of domestication and subjection, which characterized colonial rule. While freedom, liberty, and equality were the organizing principles of the new society, it was citizenship, as the repository of these principles that marked an enduring rupture from the past. This rupture entailed an emphatic creation of the collective political subject—'we the people'—as the source of authority of the constitution. The collective political subject was, moreover, not merely notional and symbolic, but was achieved consciously through what Swaminathan (2013) has called a 'deliberately designed procedural error in the adoption of the new constitution'. In order to ensure that the legal authority of the constitution could not be traced to its imperial predecessor, and the constitution could be truly *autochthonous* or indigenous, the Constituent Assembly did not adhere to the legal frameworks and modalities of transition prescribed by the Indian Independence Act of 1947. In a conscious circumvention of the procedure prescribed under the act, the constitution was not put before the British Parliament for its approval. In addition, Article 395 of the Constitution of India repealed the Indian Independence Act. The repeal of the act ensured that the rules of recognition of the constitution and its pedigree could no longer be traced to the imperial Crown-in-Parliament.

The modern state in India took the ideological and institutional form in the historical context of colonialism. The contest between the colonial state and the notions of self-determination and equality, which informed the anti-colonial struggles, provided the space for the development of modern citizenship in India. The postcolonial context was marked by the emergence of a sovereign nation state and a transformative constitutionalism, which was tasked with locating the legal sovereign. The figure of the citizen in the postcolonial moment embodied the contradictions of this transformative moment, which held out the promise of rupture from a past marked by deep social divisions and inequality, and yet remained sutured to it by the logic of the nation state and the social and political power central to the modern state.

The citizen precipitated at the originary moment of the constitution was placed at the threshold of a future unfettered by the past of colonial subjection. Yet, the citizen embodied the dialectic contradiction of the moment. This contradiction is made evident in the well-known assertion by B.R. Ambedkar that on 26 January 1950 the nation would enter into a life of contradictions represented by formal equality in the political domain alongside deeply entrenched socio-economic inequalities, which, if they endured, would imperil the Indian democracy. The description of the constituent moment by Ambedkar as a condition of a potentially imperilling paradox was distinct from Nehru's reference to it as a transcendental moment. This can be read in Nehru's 'tryst with destiny' speech and the claim that Independence symbolized the 'end of an age'. In the life of constitutional democracy in India, the contradiction between the constitutional framework of equal citizenship and actually existing inequalities has made the constitution a site of contestations that have often opened up spaces for the expansion of substantive citizenship.

The Constitutional Text and Citizenship

Citizenship is largely construed as a legal status bestowing free and equal membership in the political community. It is also, however, the source of a shared identity, which becomes the organizing principle for a sovereign nation state. The idea of citizenship as incorporated in the Indian constitution draws from the diverse struggles waged against the multiple layers of oppressive structures and discursive constructions of racial and caste superiority. These struggles enveloped all the regions of India and were, therefore, encompassing it their scale. At the same time, however, they erupted at numerous sites, acquiring distinctive forms and expressions. These struggles both in their scale and plurality of forms may be seen as aspiring to invert oppressive structures at two broad layers of collective bondage: against a hierarchically organized scheme of social relations marked by ascriptive inequalities or inequalities emerging from conditions of birth; and the domination–subjection relationship between the colonizer and the colonized.

Social relations in India were hierarchically organized, held together by ascriptive inequalities, and sustained by an unequal distribution of power. These hierarchical relations were legitimized by religious beliefs, sanctions, and ritual practices. Resistance against the entrenched feudal-brahmanical-ritual authority and its collusive dominance with colonial administrators took the form of struggles against collectively experienced humiliation. These struggles raised issues of education, respectability of social status, opportunities of occupation and vertical mobility, and improvement of economic status. Cumulatively, these struggles aspired to create a civil society, in which power relations buttressed by ascriptive hierarchies could be dismantled. The democratization of power was central to the emergence of a national–political community. The equality of all members of the political community and the idea of sovereign personhood, could eventually find formal 'affirmation' within the nation state through the notions of citizenship and territoriality.

At a pan Indian scale, struggles for the inversion of the collective subjection of Indian people took the form of a national movement for self-determination and sovereignty. Directed against the colonial state, the national movement expressed itself through a dual register. Claims for equality in the political domain were made through demands for a greater share in ruling the country, and participation in the central and provincial legislatures, and the executive councils. On the other hand, this contest also took the form of non-cooperation and civil disobedience as a political strategy of mass mobilization against colonial rule. It is significant that the form and substance of civil disobedience as articulated by Gandhi was based on a distrust of the oppressive structures of the modern state, especially its historically specific form—the colonial state—and his commitment to the moral right of the individual to rebel against unjust rule. Indeed, resisting an unjust government was at the core of Gandhi's duties of citizenship. Citizenship for Gandhi was based on the fulfilment of certain duties, and rights were conditions that followed the exercise of a citizen's duty to participate in the political process that catered to the common good. The idea was that duties and rights go together and that one cannot expect to enjoy rights, even the right to live, without subjecting oneself to obligations. The liberal ethic of resisting an unjust government as a citizen's duty is brought out in Gandhi's enunciation of the rules of civil disobedience. The political culture of jail-going, evolved by Gandhi in his war of positions with the colonizers in the 1920s and 1930s, was premised on the moral duty to resist unjust rule, which every individual possessed autonomously.

The idea of the nation as a sovereign and self-determining people emerged along the plural axes of struggles against domination. The struggle against feudal and brahmanic domination aimed at creating a political community of citizens bound by a horizontal camaraderie, which could be achieved by breaking down the ascriptive social hierarchies. The establishment of such a camaraderie of equals required not merely breaking free from the strangleholds of feudal and brahmanic domination, but also an assertion of inherent rights to one's own culture and identity. The assertion of a distinctive cultural identity became the source for laying claims to equality as a group and simultaneously the inclusion of individual members of the group into the body politic, as abstract citizens with equal civil, political, and socio-economic rights. Entry into the camaraderie of equal citizenship, promised the anonymity of liberation from ascriptive hierarchies, and consequently access to education, social mobility, protection against social indignities, and political participation. Resistance against colonial domination foregrounded the nation as the source of sovereignty of a people. The nation became then a repository of an exclusive national identity and source of sovereignty for a 'unique' people. The articulation of citizenship in such a way marked a rupture in the colonial rule of difference, with the colonized refusing to accept membership of a civil society of subjects.

The Indian constitution incorporates both these notions of citizenship—a political community assuring horizontal *camaraderie* as opposed to hierarchical inequalities, through its commitment to secure to all its citizens, justice, liberty, equality, and fraternity. The promise of equality was premised on effacing ascriptive inequalities and masking differences (of caste, gender, religion, ethnicity, and the like) making them irrelevant for citizenship. At the same time, the integrative promise of citizenship was enunciated through constitutional measures that accommodated diverse groups and communities into the political community by enumerating rights for different social groups and cultural and religious communities.

T.H. Marshall 's study has explained how citizenship developed in Britain as a bundle of rights over a period of three centuries. In the Indian context, civil, political, and social rights had a synchronous birth, through their enumeration in the constitution as the Fundamental Rights of citizens. The rights and obligations of citizens as prevalent in the nineteenth century and understood thereafter were largely seen in terms of the relationship between nation states and their *individual* members. Equality and freedom were the twin principles on which this relationship was raised. Freedom and equality, prepared the grounds for citizens to pursue their individual aims and aspirations to the best of their capacities. The conditions for full and equal enjoyment of individual rights were to be provided by the state by minimizing social and economic differences among citizens. The citizen could thus be conceived as a 'floating'/'masked' individual shorn of all characteristics of his/her social context.

The subject of rights in the Indian constitution, however, is not just the individual, but also cultural and religious communities and social groups. In the chapter on Fundamental Rights in the Constitution, Articles 14 to 24 guarantee to all citizens the rights of freedom and equality. Articles 25 to 30 in the same chapter, collectively termed 'Right to Freedom of Religion' (Articles 25 to 28) and 'Cultural and Educational Rights' (Articles 29 to 30), deal explicitly with the rights of religious and cultural communities and minority groups. It is this cluster of articles that forms the basis of the rights to equality of religious communities by empowering them to administer their civil matters through 'personal laws'. They also provide that religious communities could 'manage their own affairs in matters of religion', and for that purpose could acquire and administer property, impart religious education, preserve their language, script, culture, etc. Thus, while the masked citizen persists as the bearer of rights within the constitution, the community is also recognized as a relevant collective unit of social and political life of the nation, and seen as relevant for differentiation among citizens. Social equality could thus be defined in a way so as to assure to each community the right to be culturally different. In addition, 'differentiated-citizenship' has been incorporated in the constitution through provisions that give special protection to disadvantaged groups to erase inequalities arising out of socio-economic hierarchies of religion, caste, class, sex, and place of birth.

There would thus appear to exist within the constitution two subjects of rights, namely, the individual and the community/group, and correspondingly two languages of rights, one referring to the individual citizen and the other to the community, with the former claiming to identify individual differences, and the latter recognizing the particular contexts of different communities and groups (Menon 1998). A closer scrutiny would, however, show that there is in fact no segmentation or dichotomization, and what may appear to be individual-catering rights are in fact interwoven with a commitment to community and group rights (Larson 1997). Equal citizenship as articulated in the fundamental rights provisions of the Indian constitution combines in itself principles of non-discrimination, enjoining the state to assure to all its citizens equal protection of the law, equality of opportunity, and protection against discrimination. In other words, it ensures that the government will not discriminate against any citizen on grounds of religion, race, caste, sex, place of birth, and the like. At the same time, however, the provisions also exempt the state from adhering to 'equal treatment', by laying down that nothing in the equality provisions in the constitution will prevent the state from making special provisions for disadvantaged sections of citizens.

Articles 14 and 15 of the constitution, for example, assure equality before the law to all citizens. The right to equality is made effective by prohibiting discrimination based on caste, religion, race, etc., in order to minimize the unevenness and differences, which may emerge from social contexts. While catering to the individual, however, these rights also reserve for the state a commitment to community-ship, by recognizing that certain groups like the Scheduled Castes (SCs), Scheduled Tribes (STs), and Other Backward Classes (OBCs), were entitled to special rights. Thus Article 15 lays down that '[T]he State shall not discriminate against any citizen on grounds only of religion, race, caste, sex, place of birth or any of them' and then in clause (4) reserves for the state the right to make 'special provision for the advancement of any socially and educationally backward classes of citizens or for the Scheduled Castes and Scheduled Tribes'. Similarly Article 16, which guarantees equality of opportunity for all citizens in matters of public employment, also provides for compensatory discrimination in favour of certain communities. Thus, Article 16(2) lays down that 'no citizen shall, on grounds only of religion, race, caste, sex, descent, place of birth, residence or any of them, be ineligible for, or discriminated against in respect of, any employment or office under the State'. Article 16(4) provides the exception saying that '[N]othing in this article shall prevent the State from making any provision for the reservation of appoint-ment or posts in favour of any backward class of citizens which, in the opinion of the State, is not adequately represented in the services under the State'. Article 17 abolishes untouchability, forbidding its practice in any form and lays down that the 'enforcement of any disability arising out of "untouchability" shall be an offence punishable in accordance with law'. Article 23 prohibits traffic in human beings and 'begar' and forced labour in any form. Over and above these specific rights to equality that offer freedom from discrimination and social exclusion, and invest the state with a constitutional obligation to provide such conditions, the various rights to life enunciated and elaborated under Article 21 of the Indian constitution provide an overarching framework within which security against physical violence, equal protection under the principles of rule of law, and a substantive right to life with dignity may be assured. Constitutional provisions assuring life and security to the SCs and STs have been made legally effective through specific laws abolishing untouchability, atrocities, and discrimination.

The 'Directive Principles of State Policy' in Part IV of the Constitution contain certain non-justiciable rights. Like the Fundamental Rights, the rights in this section show a 'simultaneous commitment' to 'the rights of the community' and also of the citizens as individuals. Article 38, for example, instructs the state to 'promote the welfare of the people' by promoting a 'social order' in which 'justice, social, economic and political, shall inform all the institutions of the national life'. In order to achieve social, economic, and political justice, the state must 'strive to minimise inequalities of income' and also 'eliminate inequalities in status, facilities and opportunities'. Justice and equality is to be assured by the state, 'not only amongst individuals but also amongst groups of people residing in different areas or engaged in different vocations' (Larson 1997).

The commitment to community-ship in Articles 14 to 24 and thereafter in the Directive Principles is different from the rights of communities woven into the articles promising cultural rights to linguistic and religious communities. The rights to equality and freedom promised in Articles 14 to 24 and the Directive Principles take into consideration the exceptional circumstances of disadvantaged groups and provide for special ameliorative and affirmative rights to enable them to overcome socio-economic disabilities. While the subject of amelioration are specific socially and economically disadvantaged groups of people the purpose of the provisions is ultimately to remove the debilitating conditions so that the grounds may be prepared for the integration of an incrementally large numbers of persons into the horizontal camaraderie of citizenship. The second cluster of rights, that is, Articles 25 to 30 speak of the rights of communities, but in a different vein, since it explicitly prioritizes the cultural community, and concerns itself with its preservation. Rights in this cluster assume that cultural and religious communities are constitutive of the primary identities of individuals, which shape their needs and aspirations. As a consequence, the definition of communities in cultural terms brings some individuals, that is, those belonging to such communities, under the purview of these rights, and, therefore, makes them especially and exceptionally affected by them.

Making Good Citizens: Fundamental Duties

During the national emergency, in 1976, the Indian Parliament passed the 42nd Constitutional Amendment Act. Among the changes made by the amendment, was the insertion of Article 51A in Part IVA of the constitution. The new Article added a list of Fundamental Duties of citizens, incorporating thereby a notion of 'responsible citizenship' within the legal–constitutional framework. The duties of a citizen within the framework of a constitutional democracy, appear to instill in all citizens the consciousness that the exercise of all rights come with corresponding duties towards fellow citizens, and to the nation. In addition, rights are exercised in a social context, so that the claims to any right is constrained and also regulated by similar rights of others. For example, a person cannot by the written word, speech, or action injure the religious sentiments of another person and claim protection of the right to freedom of expression under Article 19. The duties are addressed to citizens, and do not lay down corresponding obligations on the state. This would imply that a citizen cannot claim that the state should provide the conditions that would facilitate the efficient exercise of her/his duties (*Head Masters* v. *Union of India*[1]). Unlike the fundamental rights, duties are not enforceable by mandamus or any other legal remedy (*Surya* v. *Union of India*[2]). It may be pointed out, however, that the Supreme Court has sought to make specific duties effective by issuing directions to the state to make them effective, such as Article 51A(g) which enjoins the citizens to 'protect and improve the natural environment including forests, lakes, rivers, and wild life, and to have compassion for living creatures' (*Rural Litigation* v.

[1] AIR 1983 Cal 448, 87 CWN 597.
[2] AIR 1982 Raj 1, 1981 WLN 198.

State of U.P.;[3] *Sachidanand* v. *State of West Bengal;*[4] *Mehta* v. *Union of India*[5] [Basu 1999: 311]). The Supreme Court can also uphold as reasonable, any law seeking to prohibit the violation of Fundamental Duties, even if the law restricted a Fundamental Right. This can be derived from the attitude of the court towards the implementation of provisions of Part IV of the constitution and the belief, even before the insertion of a separate list of duties, that Part IV of the constitution, that is, the directives, demanded certain obligations from the citizens. In *Chandra Bhavan* v. *State of Mysore,*[6] for example, the Supreme Court decided that 'it [was] a fallacy to think that under our constitution there are only rights and no duties. The provisions in Part IV enable the Legislatures to impose various duties on the citizens. The mandate of our constitution is to build a welfare society and that object may be achieved to the extent the Directive Principles are implemented by legislation' (Basu 1999: 310). The inclusion of duties

[3] (1985) INSC 220.

[4] (1987) 2 SCC 295.

[5] 1988 AIR 1115 1988 SCR (2) 530.

[6] AIR 1970 SC 2042.

in the constitution, it may be argued, has introduced a principle of active and responsible citizenship in the constitutional text. While there may not exist a provision in the constitution that makes the duties enforceable, their implementation or dissemination through pedagogical practices may be seen as reasonable in law.

The list of ten Fundamental Duties were inserted during the 42nd constitutional amendment. The list gives us an insight into what might constitute 'good' citizenship under the constitution. Some of the duties may be seen as segmented into different categories, invoking distinct corresponding notions of citizenship. A section exhorts citizens to strive towards 'excellence', develop a 'scientific temper' and safeguard 'public property', and appears to instil civility and civic citizenship. Civic citizenship is also promoted through certain secular idioms and invocation of symbols of constitutional patriotism. Every citizen of India is exhorted *to respect symbols of national unity* like the national flag, the constitution, and the national anthem, and *sources of common heritage* like the 'national struggle for freedom' and the tradition of 'composite culture'. There is, however, also a tendency towards ethnic citizenship, through the instillation of a sense of national unity and integration and a simultaneous requirement of strengthening the state. Consequently, citizens are expected to preserve the 'sovereignty' and 'unity' of the country by pledging to 'defend' the country, offer 'national service' and spread a feeling of 'common brotherhood'.

In the struggle for national liberation, 'citizenship' was inextricably associated with the articulation of a distinctive national identity as the basis of assertion for equality (with the colonizer) and the claims for rights (as indicative of autonomous and sovereign selfhood). An incipient civic ideal essential for building a public morality consonant with citizenship can, however, also be traced. 'Institutions, habits, activities and spirit' by 'means' of which 'a man or a woman may fulfill the duties and receive the benefits of membership' was considered integral to the study of Civics in colleges and universities. It was common for universities and Intermediate Examination Boards, for example, the Calcutta University examinations of 1927 and 1930 and the United Provinces Intermediate Board examinations of 1928 and 1930, to focus on the definition, scope, and meaning of citizenship. The importance of Civics as a discipline lay in 'preparing' students for 'citizenship'. In Mihir Kumar Sen's book, *Elements of*

Civics, the 14th edition of which was printed in 1946, the citizen forms the nucleus surrounded by concentric circles of social and political existence, innermost being the family, followed by the village, the city, the country, and the outermost, the empire. Sen suggests that *Indian* citizenship was, however, a limited one, because of the absence of certain (civil) liberties. Surprisingly, Sen does not see the roots of truncated citizenship in India in the colonial condition, and finds the explanation for its restricted nature in the general pattern of the history of India, in which India had always been part of an empire or had empires within and where only members of the conquering race enjoyed citizenship. The contemporary context of the British colonialism was, however, by Sen seen as offering different possibilities of citizenship, since the British Empire comprised 'autonomous parts'. Citizenship in India, thought Sen, could be realized through 'Dominion status'—in being a 'citizens of the empire'—whereby, Indians would not only have Indian citizenship, but would simultaneously stand at par with citizens of other parts of the empire (Sen 1946: 83–4).

The idea of citizenship as equality within the empire was modified by legal experts like V.S. Srinivas Sastri who delivered a series of lectures in 1926—the Kamala Lectures on the Rights and Duties of the Indian Citizen—in Calcutta and Madras. The lectures are available in an edited volume published in 1948. While exhorting for 'the education of every man [sic] ... into alert citizenship and the ways of Reason, justice and dignified human relations', Sastri appeals to the 'leaders' to 'build this *constructive* citizenship slowly and surely on the foundations of *ordered* progress' (Sastri 1948: 5). While it is not clear who are the leaders Sastri refers to, his discomfort with the 'nationalist' methods of change, are evident in his appeal to the 'law-breaker' 'I recognise that there are situations in which one has the right to break the law, but please remember that there are others less law abiding than yourself who will see your precedent and make the extreme medicine of the constitution its daily bread.' (Sastri 1948: 5–6).

His lecture on 'Duties of Citizens', where Sastri addresses his 'fellow-citizens, brothers [sic] in a growing citizenship' shows a similar tendency of distrust with what he calls 'worse alternatives' that feature 'in our inherited tendency'. This inherited tendency 'to over-throw', and 'to disestablish', he cautions has ushered in 'a state of anarchy in the country', destroying 'order and ordered government'. In addition, the *revolutionary* and *anarchical* forces now afoot', he warns, have made even 'our best men' disinclined towards performing their duties as leaders responsibly (Sastri 1948: 86–7).

Unlike Shastri, Gandhi placed the moral right to rebel and resist an unjust government at the core of the 'duties of citizenship'. In his war of positions with the colonizers, Gandhi crafted a political culture of jail-going in the 1920s and 1930s, which was embedded in the moral duty to resist. This duty, that all individuals possessed autonomously, made it '... wrong to be free under a government [held] to be wholly bad'. The moral duty to resist was made manifest in the civil resistance or *satyagrahi*'s quest for truth and freedom, who defied a 'bad' government by breaking unjust laws, and voluntarily embracing imprisonment as a punishment. When punished, the rules of satyagraha expected the satyagrahi prisoner to be 'strictly correct', 'dignified', 'submissive' to the punishment regime, and show no disregard for prison discipline except under extraordinary circumstances of 'gross inhumanity' and 'indignity'. The adherence to prison discipline was explained by Gandhi through the logic of civil disobedience. If the person breaking laws voluntarily also violated the sanctions that followed the breach, she/he ceased to be civil (a citizen) and became anarchic (Singh 1998: 74–8).

In his speech in the Constituent Assembly of India on 25 November 1949,[7] that is, a day before the constitution was adopted, B.R. Ambedkar proposed a framework for ensuring the stability of constitutional democracy. Arguing that the primary concern of a citizen in a democracy should be to preserve the constitutional edifice of democracy which had been built so painstakingly, Ambedkar made a case for 'holding fast' onto the constitutional methods of achieving social and economic objectives before the nation. The 'bloody methods of revolution', indeed, the methods of 'civil disobedience, non-cooperation and satyagraha', he suggested, should be abandoned. These methods, he argued, could be justified only in those contexts where constitutional methods of social change were not available. This was no longer the case in India. Wherever constitutional methods were present, these

[7] Speech of B.R. Ambedkar, Constituent Assembly Debates, 25 November 1949. The debates are available online at http://parliamentofindia.nic.in/ls/debates/debates.htm (last accessed 5 April 2016).

methods were 'nothing but the Grammar of Anarchy'. In addition, Ambedkar cautioned against the path of 'bhakti', 'hero worship', and devotion emerging out of gratitude in politics, which amounted to laying down one's liberties at the feet of a man—'trusting him with power which enables him to subvert their institutions'. While in religion, bhakti could be a road to salvation, in politics it was 'a sure road to degradation and eventual dictatorship'. Ambedkar further advises vigilance against complacency and contentment with 'mere political democracy'. On 26 January 1950, he cautioned, India would enter into 'a life of contradictions' where equality in the political domain would coexist with inequalities in the social and economic life. This contradiction, if not addressed expeditiously, would imperil political democracy (CAD, 25 November 1949).

In 1999, a committee was set up by the Government of India under the chairpersonship of Justice J.S. Verma to suggest the ways by which fundamental duties mentioned in the Indian constitution could be taught through the school curriculum. The report titled, 'Fundamental Duties of Citizens: Report of the Committee to Operationalize the Suggestions to Teach

Fundamental Duties to the Citizens of the Country', submitted by the Justice Verma Committee made the publicity of the Preamble of the Constitution along with the Fundamental Duties one of its salient recommendations. Under the head 'Generating Awareness and Consciousness', the report emphasized that the purpose of the recommendations was to remind every individual that 'citizenship is a solemn duty which every individual must discharge with due diligence and dedication', especially in the 'current conjecture of social, economic and political forces' that call for 'a *movement* which captures the imagination of masses and motivates all categories of citizens' (Ministry of Human Resource Development 1999; emphasis added).[8] While school textbooks had, for quite some

[8] The Committee was set up by the Ministry of Human Resource Development on 21 July 1998 in response to a notice issued to the Government of India by the Supreme Court of India on 18 March 1998 on the basis of a letter dated 18 March 1998 from Justice Rangnath Mishra (former Chief Justice of India). The letter was treated by the Supreme Court as a writ petition to enquire into the ways in which the government envisaged the operationalization of constitutional values to generate a duty-bound society necessary for nation building.

time, carried the Preamble of the Constitution in their opening pages, all books now open to both the Preamble and Fundamental Duties, occluding the fact that Fundamental Duties are not synchronous with the Preamble. The Fundamental Duties were a later addition, inserted in the constitution by the 42nd Amendment during the Emergency, when the Parliament had been purged of political opposition, public discussions and debates were stifled, and basic rights of citizens were curtailed. Thus, what went into the constitution as the Fundamental Duties of Citizens, without critical public inputs and debates, forms the basis of teaching in school curriculum and elsewhere.

The Verma Committee Report (MHRD 1999) on its part, sought to 'operationalize' duties by proposing that an *Indian* identity should provide the foundation upon which the identity of a *cosmopolitan* Indian could be constructed, based on the retention of the specificity of the national in relation to the world. Coming to terms with a globalized world where nation states/ national boundaries/national cultures were becoming pervious to influences from outside, appeared to be a predominant concern. An anxiety around retrieving and preserving a pure national identity embedded in an Indian culture is reflected in the report, in the prioritization of an Indian way of life and evolving a Universal Declaration of Human Responsibilities that recognizes the supremacy of Eastern thought (MHRD 1999: 7–8). While emphasizing that the duties are just a 'codification of tasks integral to an Indian way of life', and that a number of clauses of Article 51A 'basically refer to such values as have been a part of the Indian tradition, mythology, religions, and practice', the report breaks up the duties enumerated in the constitution into three according to the target group they cater to: the 'nation' as a whole, the 'community', and the 'individual'. The expected learning outcomes of 'a deliberate programme of education in Fundamental Duties' were 'understanding, appreciation and action' and although this involved, as the report rightly said, a 'wide range of cognitive levels', it considered it important to focus on textbooks since in most cases they were the sole source of teaching.

While there is nothing wrong with inculcating citizenship values through textbooks, it is the association of citizen's duties with the development of national pride/consciousness/dignity and identity that strikes a dissonant note. The debates that followed in the wake of the revision of social studies textbooks, history textbooks in particular, show that the processes by which national pride and dignity are sought reflect the hegemonic impulses of the ruling regimes. While this impulse is not conspicuous in the report itself, a silence on how the duties catering to the target group 'nation', including 'cherishing the values of the national movement' may actually be open to exclusionary tendencies homogenizing the target group itself, becomes significant. The association of citizen's duties with a hegemonically conceived national identity makes for a passive and thin notion of citizenship. In this context, even the remaining clauses that cater to community-ship, and individual and collective excellence, become limited in their scope and content.

It may be emphasized here that a substantial body of recent scholarship on citizenship, irrespective of ideo-logical divides, thinks it necessary to concentrate on the notion of citizenship as a function of 'responsible' participation. There is thus a growing emphasis on 'citizenship as activity' (as distinct from citizenship as status and entitlements) as the basis of a citizen's membership in the political community. The good citizen produced merely for purposes of governance, prioritizes stability at the expense of democracy. In the present scenario where the influence of political conservatism has prioritized descent and ethnic origin as the basis of political identity of citizenship, and neo-liberals have prioritized the market as the school that trains citizens in qualities of excellence and achievement, it is important to examine the idea of citizen's duties carefully, especially if such duties have constitutional status and the potential, therefore, for legal enforcement carrying penalties for non-compliance. It must be borne in mind that within specific political contexts, duties may be interpreted in ways that are harmful and detrimental to certain groups, especially since there is an absence of a corresponding constitutional duty of the state to provide conditions in which citizens may be able to discharge their duties. Moreover, contrary to the assertion that the constitution has ushered in a rights-oriented society, the constitution has been experienced differentially by different sections of people. Apart from the fact that the actualization of rights that are guaranteed in the constitution depend on the class, caste, religion, gender, and sexuality of the rights-bearing citizen, the constitution itself permits and provides the procedure for their amendment and abridgment by the state.

In this context it is important to note that in Chapter 10 where the Report makes its 'salient recommendations', it considers it appropriate to take recourse to the 'punitive provisions of the law' along with 'social sanctions' and 'exemplar role models' to operationalize duties (Verma Committee Report 1999: 46). Insofar as historically, and especially in the course of the national liberation movement which the duties also mention, if citizenship has endured as the means as well as the condition of freedom, it seems anachronistic to associate it with penal sanctions. The attempt to attach penal sanctions to duties seems indicative of an anxiety with the churning processes in a society in transition, reminiscent of Srinivasa Sastri's apprehensions about the disruption in 'ordered progress', and Gandhi and Ambedkar's concerns around its degradation into anarchy. In political traditions where citizenship was inextricably associated with notions of civic virtue and efficient performance of duty, the political community was conceived differently, with no 'them and us' distinction/opposition of government and the governed. In modern societies where such a difference does exist, and the emphasis is on freedom through liberation from traditional/iniquitous obligations, a notion of morality of the community founded on principles of justice and reasonableness, has persisted. Such a morality requires that the citizen must not only be eternally vigilant of the government, but also engage in activities of protest, including civil disobedience. While harmony, concord, and community are significant ingredients of active citizenship, it is important to re-examine the idea of duties as it exists in the constitution, asking oneself at the same time, to whom the list is addressed, whether its contents are actually essential for making good citizens, whether at all they should be part of the constitution, and whether they have the capacity to usher in a civil society where democracy is nurtured as a civic virtue.

Constitutional Morality and the Elaboration of Citizenship

In the legal ensemble of citizenship as laid down in the text of the constitution and the statutory framework in the Citizenship Act of 1955, citizenship relies on practices that make citizens legible. Legibility in turn pertains to measurable and identifiable categories such as duration of residence, facts about domicile, dates of entry and departure, birth, lineage/descent, and so on. These identifiers are in turn made dependent on, draw upon, and correspond to significant moments in the life of the nation and the imperatives of locating the legal sovereign amidst as Upendra Baxi says, 'prior [and continuing] histories of power and struggle [which] shape the project of writing a constitution and the specific modes of governance and production of juridical norms' (Baxi 2008: 93). The legal ensemble, moreover, depicts an interactive relationship between the constitution, law, and the ongoing state formative practices.

The constitution may be seen as made up of dual and mutually contradictory registers, which generate different logics and tendencies. One of these is the citizenship and rights register, which owes its origin to the national liberation struggles, and corresponds with the logic of democracy. The governance register, on the other hand, occupies a disproportionately large space in the constitutional text, and is seen as carrying forward the logic of bureaucracy put in place by the colonial state (Kaviraj 2003). The democratic register, unlike the bureaucratic register, is construed as marking the creative and inaugural moment of the modern state in India. It is in this register that democratic churnings are witnessed in postcolonial India, which then becomes the site for the expansion of citizenship.

The notion of constitutional morality was invoked by the constitutional framers while laying down the structures of the administrative and institutional apparatus of the state—the ponderously meticulous details of the organization of the governmental apparatus. Pratap Mehta explains constitutional morality, following Grote, as 'a paramount reverence for the forms of government' and 'obedience to authority', which requires conformity with prescribed norms. Yet, conformity also needs to be combined with 'the habit of open-speech' and 'unrestrained censure' of those in authority. Speech and censure are, however, not unbridled but always subject to legal restraint, and eventually to the 'preponderant sacredness of the constitution' (Mehta 2010: 16–17). The appeal to constitutional morality is often made to instil adherence to a mode of association in which self-restraint is a precondition for 'maintaining freedom under properly constituted conditions' (Mehta 2010: 18). On

4 November 1948, speaking in the Constituent Assembly on 'The Draft Constitution', Ambedkar stressed the importance of the diffusion of constitutional morality in the entire community as an indispensable condition for a free government. Quite like his elaboration of constitutional morality in a speech made later in the Constituent Assembly on 25 November 1949, for Ambedkar, self-restraint was an essential requirement for achieving social change: freedom and democracy could be sustained only through 'constitutional methods' of achieving the objectives of social and economic change. In such a framework of constitutional morality, it was not just the revolutionary method that was rendered redundant and excessive, but also civil disobedience, non-cooperation, and satyagraha.

In his discussion of the Delhi High Court judgement in the *Naz Foundation* case[9], Upendra Baxi (2011) reads the judgement as having developed a notion of constitutional morality, which gave a fuller meaning to

---

[9] *Naz Foundation* v. *Government of New Capital Territory of Delhi and Others*, Delhi Law Times vol. 160 (2009) (hereinafter referred to as *Naz Foundation*).

the idea of dignity. The judgement came in response to
an appeal by the Naz Foundation and Others against
Section 377 of the IPC, which had been used to
criminalize same-sex relationships. Section 377 of the
Indian Penal Code prescribes a punishment of a fine
or imprisonment for a term of ten years or to life, for
'unnatural offences'. It defines an unnatural offence as
'carnal intercourse against the order of nature with any
man, woman or animal'. Deciding in favour of scrapping Section 377, Justices A.P. Shah and S. Muralidhar
argued that the right to privacy was integral to the
right to live with dignity, and gave it worth as a moral
and juridical idea. To read a right to dignity in the
constitution, the judges invoked a notion of constitutional morality, which was not about self-restraint
as a condition of freedom, but which referred to an
'amplitude of free choice ... the modes of creating
and being in a world of one's own choosing'. For
the judges, parts III, IV, and IV-A of the constitution
provide the threshold of critical morality, to be used
as evaluative standards for judging public morality. In
a nuanced articulation, the *Naz Foundation* insisted
that constitutional morality derived from the basic
constitutional values, which alone provided valid

justification for the restriction of the fundamental right to life. They argued: 'If there is any type of "morality" that can pass the test of compelling state interest, it must be "constitutional" morality and not public morality' (*Naz Foundation*, para 79). This meant that in *no* event, can 'moral indignation, howsoever strong' provide any 'valid basis for overriding individual's fundamental rights of dignity and privacy. In our scheme of things, constitutional morality must outweigh the argument of public morality, even if it be the majoritarian view' (*Naz Foundation*, para 86).

Often, however, the courts have been ambivalent and have endorsed the political closure of rights. Several signposts are, however, identifiable where judicial interpretations have given new and more expansive meanings to fundamental rights, enhancing differentiated citizenship. Variegated interpretations of Article 21 of the constitution have effectively made it the repository of meanings, which take it far beyond its enumeration as protection of life and personal liberty. The elaboration of the right to life in the *Naz Foundation* judgement was achieved through a scrutiny of the heteronormative universe of citizenship and the silence it spun over questions of sexuality. While homosexuality and the 'queer citizen' is the 'invisible subject' of civil law, she/he is the 'hyper-visible' (Narrain 2007: 61) subject of criminal law. Used to criminalize homosexuality, Section 377 was evaluated in *Naz Foundation* against the standards of constitutional morality, found wanting, and repealed. Scholars like Upendra Baxi have seen the principles enunciated by Justices Shah and Muralidhar in the *Naz Foundation* judgement as having produced a new jurisprudence of equality that promised emancipation from the culture of stigmatization co-produced by the state and society. An appeal against the Delhi High Court judgement resulted in the Supreme Court ruling against the scrapping of Section 377, asking the courts to exercise self-restraint while deciding in matters concerning constitutionality of laws, and leaving it to the Parliament to decide whether it was desirable to amend or retain Section 377. The extraction of Section 377 from the judicial domain and its relocation in the legislative domain, meant a failure to retrieve and consolidate the exceptional moment opened up by the Naz judgement to subject the archaic IPC to the scrutiny of contemporary constitutional interpretation.

The space for the articulation of a judicially inno-
vated constitutional right opened up earlier in *Olga
Tellis* v. *Bombay Municipal Corporation*[10] (BMC) decided
in August 1985. In this case the Supreme Court
affirmed that there existed a relationship between life,
livelihood, and the dwelling place. The petitioners in
this case were pavement and slum dwellers in Bombay
(joined by the People's Union for Civil Liberties,
Committee for the Protection of Democratic Rights,
and journalists), who had migrated to Bombay
around 1960–1, and had been evicted by the State of
Maharashtra and the BMC for having encroached on
public spaces. The petitioners challenged the demolition of their dwellings by the BMC in the Bombay
High Court. The high court ruled that the petitioners
could not claim a fundamental right to put up huts
on pavements or public roads, asking them to vacate
the huts by 15 October 1981. In their appeal to the
Supreme Court challenging the High Court ruling,
the petitioners argued that demolition of pavement
dwellings and the slum hutments deprived them

[10] AIR 1986 SC 180.

of the right to livelihood guaranteed by Article 21 of the constitution and that it was constitutionally impermissible to characterize the pavement dwellers as 'trespassers', because their occupation of pavements arose from economic compulsions. The Supreme Court judgement wavered between recognizing the compulsions in the lives of migrant workers, the 'filth and squalor' in the slums and pavements dwellings, and the failure of the city's master plan to take into account the need to redistribute the city-space, and on the other hand, acknowledging that it was the BMC's duty to reclaim public spaces for what the court saw as legitimate public use. After painstakingly weaving the right to livelihood into the fundamental right to life, and their critical relationship with the right to a dwelling, the judges stopped short of recognizing the petitioner's claims to public spaces in the city. They held instead that 'the procedure prescribed by law for depriving a person of his fundamental right, in this case the right to life' conformed to the 'norms of justice and fair play', but also instructed the state government to 'make good' its various assurances of rehabilitating the evicted petitioners. Ten years later, in *Chameli*

Singh and Others v. *State of U.P. and Another*,[11] decided in 1996, a bench of three judges of the Supreme Court held that the right to shelter was a fundamental right available to all citizens, and they read it as encompassed by Article 21, making the right to life more meaningful:

> In any organised society, right to live as a human being is not ensured by meeting only the animal needs of man. It is secured only when he is assured of all facilities to develop himself and is freed from restrictions which inhibit his growth.... Right to shelter, therefore, includes adequate living space, safe and decent structure, clean and decent surroundings, sufficient light, pure air and water, electricity, sanitation and other civic amenities like roads etc. so as to have easy access to his daily avocation. The right to shelter, therefore, does not mean a mere right to a roof over one's head but right to all the infrastructure necessary to enable them to live and develop as human being. *Right to shelter when used as an essential requisite to the right to live should be deemed to have been guaranteed as a fundamental right.*

[11] (1996) 2 SCC 549.

In the same year, in *Ahmedabad Municipal Corporation v. Nawab Khan Ghulab Khan and Others*,[12] decided on 11 October 1996, the Supreme Court admitted an appeal against the Gujarat High Court's decision to put a stay on the removal of 'encroachments by pavement dwellers in unauthorized occupation of footpaths of the Rakhial Road in Ahmedabad, a main road of the city'. Quite like the *Olga Tellis* case, the Supreme Court decided:

It would, therefore, be clear that though no person has a right to encroach and erect structures or otherwise on footpath, pavement or public streets or any other place reserved or earmarked for a public purpose, the State has the Constitutional duty to provide adequate facilities and opportunities by distributing its wealth and resources for settlement of life and erection of shelter over their heads to make the right to life meaningful, effective and fruitful. Right to live [sic] livelihood is meaningful because no one can live without means of his living, that is the means of livelihood. The deprivation of the right to life in that context would not only denude right of the effective

[12] (1997) 11 SCC 123.

content and meaningfulness but it would make life miserable and impossible to live. It would, therefore, be the duty of the State to provide right to shelter to the poor and indigent weaker sections of the society in fulfillment of the Constitutional objectives.

The court also directed the Municipal Corporation to observe its 'constitutional and statutory duty' to provide means for settlement and residence by allotting the surplus land under the Urban Land Ceiling Act and if necessary by acquiring land and providing house sites or tenements, as the case may be, according to the scheme formulated by the Corporation, and by evolving appropriate schemes.

In the course of articulating the rights of the worker who migrated to the city in search of a livelihood and found a dwelling on the pavements or in the slums, in both cases the Supreme Court did two things—it enlarged the scope of the right to life, but at the same time, hedged it with a pre-existing limit of 'the procedure established by law'. Thus the two municipal corporations were seen by the court to have acted in accordance with their legal duties in removing encroachments from public land. It is interesting that in neither of the two judgements the expression encroachment was used in a way so as to impute an intention (of encroaching) onto the slum and pavement dwellers. On the other hand, encroachment emerges as a condition and an outcome of a series of compelling circumstances in the life of a migrant worker. Moreover, while justifying the removal of encroachments, the court instructed the Municipal Corporations of Bombay and Ahmedabad, and the two state governments, at length, on the various programmes of rehabilitation that were to be made available to the migrant worker upon eviction. Yet, in both the judgements the court also chastised the municipal bodies for having *allowed the encroachment to endure long enough to make it the basis for a claim for rehabilitation.*

In the years that followed, public interest litigation by residents' welfare groups from middle-class colonies pulled up their respective state governments for failing to free public spaces of 'encroachments'. The Supreme Court upheld their appeals and instructed the governments to remove encroachments, but for reasons different from those given in the earlier cases. Unlike the earlier judgements, where the court saw 'encroachment' as an inadvertent consequence of migration in search of livelihood, and an aspect of the vulnerability of the migrant, in its decisions upholding petitions by environment and resident welfare groups, the Supreme Court gave centrality to the *illegality* of encroachment, dissociating it from its sociological contexts. In a Public Interest Litigation in *Almitra H. Patel* v. *Union of India*[13] the Supreme Court ordered the Delhi government and other authorities to remove 'slums and unauthorized colonies' on public land, dispossessing an estimated 35 lakh people. The court termed the slum dwellers 'encroachers' whose 'illegitimate' claim to land in compensation for dispossession from their jhuggis amounted to 'pickpocketing' the tax payer: '(t)he promise of free land at the tax payers' cost, in place of a jhuggi is a proposal which attracts many land grabbers. Rewarding an encroacher on public land with a free alternate site is like giving a reward to a pickpocket'.

In some cases, the courts have elaborated constitutional morality to make a strident critique of the coercive state apparatus, such as the deployment by the Chhattisgarh state government of young men from

[13] (2000) 2 SCC 679.

the local community as Special Police Officers (SPOs). The SPOs have become crucial in the state's war against armed resistance in Chhattisgarh, West Bengal, Orissa, Manipur, and Jammu and Kashmir. As 'insiders' to the community, the SPOs know the language and the terrain, they are familiar with the adversaries and their strategies, and most importantly, are indistinguishable from them. In Chhattisgarh, for example, the existence of large tracts of areas under Maoist control has caused anxiety in the state government regarding establishing 'access' to these areas and its command over them. The government has sought to achieve its control through the invocation of the provisions of a colonial law, the Indian Police Act (IPA), 1861. Recourse to the IPA in independent India is not merely an aspect of the extension of the state's sovereignty to inaccessible areas, it is also a means of expanding the state's power and reconfiguring the conditions within which power is exercised. Section 17 of the IPA (1861) provides for the recruitment and deployment of SPOs, empowering the local magistrate 'to *temporarily appoint civilians* as SPOs to perform the roles of "ordinary officers of police"' (emphasis added). It must be noted that the IPA (1861) predates the Criminal Procedure Code

(CrPC) and the IPC, and Section 17 may be seen as anticipating and filling in for provisions like Sections 107 of CrPC and 144 of IPC, which deal with breach of peace and unlawful assembly. Providing the legal basis for the recruitment of SPOs, the IPA (1861) is reflective of the logic of the colonial state to maintain rule by force and to elicit habitual obedience from the subject population. In its contemporary usage, however, the deployment of SPOs has become an integral part of the strategy of state governments for combating armed groups.

The Chhattisgarh government started implementing the SPO programme around June 2005. The Chhattisgarh Police Act (CPA) was enacted by the state government in 2007 making it the authoritative legal framework pertaining to the police force in the state. The substitution of IPA (1861) with the CPA (2007) resulted in the consolidation of some aspects of the colonial law and also the introduction of certain innovations. The experience from Chhattisgarh has shown that the deployment of tribal youth from the community from among those displaced by violence from the Maoists and the Salwa Judum (a civilian militia organized by the state to counter Maoist activities), as well as from the ranks of former Maoists and Salwa Judum members, has been done ostensibly on grounds of efficacy and utility. The question of efficiency pertains to matters of logistics (movement of forces) and local knowledge, especially of the forest terrain, and intimate knowledge of the community. At a deeper level, however, this deployment has aggravated the fault lines within the community, accentuated violence, and opened up new frontiers for the intrusion of the state in the local community. In a petition seeking the Supreme Court's intervention against the Salwa Judum operation (*Nandini Sundar and Others* v. *State of Chhattisgarh*[14]), the court ruled that the state of Chhattisgarh had violated the fundamental rights to life and equality of the tribal youth by failing to mitigate their 'rage, hurt and vengeance' against 'the violence perpetrated against them, or their kith and kin'. Indeed, the court argued the state had aggravated the violence by directing the tribal youth into 'counter-insurgency activities'. In addition, the court issued a

[14] W.P. (Civil) No. 250 of 2007, Supreme Court of India order of 18 January 2011.

stern indictment of the neo–liberal development policies of the state—the 'predatory forms of capitalism,
supported and promoted by the state in direct con-
travention of constitutional norms and values, [which]
often take deep roots around the extractive industries',
and constituted the backdrop of the sufferings of
tribal people.

Extension of constitutional citizenship through
judicial interpretation has also been accompanied by
laws, which have elaborated specific constitutional
provisions. Article 17 of the constitution, for example,
found legal enforcement in the Protection of Civil
Rights Act, 1955 followed by the SC/ST (Prevention
of Atrocities) Act, 1989 (henceforth SC/ST PoA Act)
amended in 2015, which prescribed severe penalties
against a series of crimes listed as atrocities against the
SCs and STs. The SC/ST PoA Act provides for the
setting up of special courts with enhanced and overriding powers to try cases under the act. While the
Civil Rights Act had approached the concerns around
discrimination in terms of socially enforced disabilities,
the SC/ST PoA Act identified a range of crimes against
the SC and ST communities as 'atrocities'. It thereby

acknowledged the violent and systemic nature of the repression faced by Dalits and tribal communities in a host of situations. Both laws, moreover, emphasize the fact that disabilities and repressions are deeply embedded in society, which, even when they make themselves manifest through specific incidents, are imposed by a dominant group and experienced collectively by the other. The limitations of constitutional provisions and their legal enforcement are seen, however, in most cases of atrocities. The Khairlanji case has perhaps become the most emblematic of this. The Bhotmanges were a Dalit family of Khairlanji in Maharashtra, owning a small plot of land. They had resisted attempts by the dominant sections of the village to construct a road through this land. On 29 September 2006, a mob of villagers attacked them while Bhaiyyalal, the father, was away. Bhaiyyalal's sons were killed and so were his wife Surekhi and daughter Priyanka, after being raped. The report on the Khairlanji killings brought out by the Centre for Equity and Social Justice of the government's Yashwantrao Chavan Academy of Development Administration (YASHDA) and the Dr Babasaheb Ambedkar Research and Training

Institute, Department of Social Justice, Government of India, found a '*deep rooted social conspiracy* toward facilitating the crime and subsequent suppressing of evidence on the part of certain communal forces as well as various elements from politics and administration' (emphasis added). It is not surprising that the case was eventually tried outside the purview of the SC/ST PoA Act manifesting the manner in which dominant social groups and political forces may render constitutional safeguards and legal protections ineffective.

As a legal status and as the organizing principle for a sovereign nation and democratic political community citizenship was incorporated in the Indian constitution through a set of rights and duties. The fundamental rights in the constitution are an outcome of the variegated struggles for self-determination waged against multilayered structures of oppression. Within the constitutional text they lay down the promise of equal citizenship for all members of the political community. The scope of citizenship has been enlarged through processes of elaboration of the constitutional text. In this context, both judicial interpretations and statutory interventions have contributed to the enhancement of citizenship. Yet, the constitutional text has been both a resource for democratic citizenship as well as the site of contestations. There have been moments in the life of constitutional democracy in India when rights have become more entrenched through judicial and legislative interventions. But there also exists a corresponding history of the judiciary and the legislature, independently or in concert, constraining the rights of citizens. The most recent illustration of this was the Supreme Court of India upholding the constitutionality of the Haryana Panchayati Raj (Amendment) Act, 2015. The judgement upheld the five additional disqualifications laid down by the act to exclude those who had criminal charges framed against them, were without a specified minimum educational qualification, in debt, did not have a functional toilet in their homes, and had arrears of electricity bills, from contesting Panchayat elections. The burden of argument in the judgement was to establish that franchise as a constitutional right was a lesser right, which is to say it was not a fundamental right, and, therefore, not entitled to the same protection as a fundamental right. The judgement effectively created two classes of citizen, one that could vote but not govern and the other that could do both, reducing franchise to a mere statutory privilege, subject to the whims of those in political power. It is at these moments that Ambedkar's warning of contradictions in Indian democracy ring poignantly true.

3

Ambivalent Citizens

There are about 50,000 people living in India as those evicted from Chitmahals. Mainly scattered over eastern India and the border regions of northeastern India, they recall torture by Bangladeshi elements, which forced them out of their land. Their horror stories remain undocumented and unheard. Sushil Rai, 57, was driven out of his Chit number 34, Behuladanga, in 1973. Rai said: 'Elements from Bangladesh would come and take away my crop. They would steal my cattle too. Nobody would come forward to help us as the Bangladeshi police also participated in the looting. In such a situation we were left with no option but to leave.' Sushil Rai now collects boulders from the dry bed of the Teesta river in the summer months. This fetches him an average income of Rs 600 a month to feed a family of 12. He said: 'After coming to the

Indian mainland nobody has come to help us. The government thinks that we are from Bangladesh. This is not true. But nobody has cared to verify the facts. My children don't go to school and I have no access to ration shops as I don't have proof that I am a resident of India.' (Kaur 2002)

Citizenship as legal membership in the nation state is inextricably associated with the corresponding figure of the outsider. Indeed, the identification of the outsider is essential for the definition of those who belong. Legal citizenship may then be seen as existing alongside the 'constitutive outsiders' or the non-citizen others, who are indispensable for affirming the citizen's identity. Denoting differential or layered membership in the political community, 'otherness' is not a relationship of 'simple opposition', which pertains to exclusion. In postcolonial theory, the relationship between the self and the other is not one of opposition or exclusion. As the Lacanian term 'forclusion' used by Gayatri Chakravarty Spivak and other postcolonial theorists conveys, it is a relationship of constant comparison so that the other is constantly implied in the identity and unity of the self. As a constant referent, the outsider is indispensable for the identification of the citizen. Ironically, like the citizen's 'virtual' image, the outsider is tied to the 'objective' citizen without, however, being able to reproduce himself/herself as one. This relationship is reproduced and reinscribed continually through legal and judicial pronouncement, so much so that the 'other' constantly cohabits the citizen's space in a relationship of incongruity. The expression 'ambivalent citizen' is being invoked in this chapter to meander through some of these sites of incongruous cohabitation.

The Nowhere People

Citizenship at the commencement of the republic was woven into the narrative of the drawing of national borders and the affirmation of state sovereignty over the territorial boundaries of the nation state. Both of these required a simultaneous legal statement of who could be designated a member of the nation state. The legal-constitutional frameworks of citizenship recognized citizens as those who resided within the national borders, or crossed them in ways that could be considered legitimate by the state. Yet, the citizenship law did not capture all the contexts in which migration across borders took place, and certain forms of movement could be brought within the purview of law only by marking them out as exceptions. One of the ways in which such cross-border movement was made legible by the state was to look at it as 'displacement'.

Unlike 'abducted persons', which was a legal category, 'displaced persons' was an administrative category. The introduction of this category gave the government the authority to represent the migration of specific groups of people across borders as displacement, opening up the possibility of new modalities of bureaucratic action. Communications among officials in the years immediately after the partition reveal that it was the Hindu minority groups migrating to India who were to be construed as displaced persons. Their legal absorption into Indian citizenship was to be facilitated through their expeditious registration as citizens, and their urgent inclusion in the electoral rolls in time for the second general election. The Ministries of Home, External Affairs, Rehabilitation, Law, and the Election Commission of India, acted in concert to make all the necessary arrangements to complete the registration of displaced persons as Indian citizens. Assurances were given in Parliament that the registration of such

117

persons would be done with the least inconvenience to them. This meant making arrangements for their registration in all places where they resided in reasonably large numbers, that is, towns, villages, refugee camps, or settlements.

A note on the instructions issued to the state governments was circulated for discussion among the officials of the Home Ministry. The note directed that exception to the Citizenship Act and Rules must be made, and strict adherence to the requirement of documentary evidence waived, to treat the displaced persons as a separate category:

> ... the persons about whom the present reference has been made belong to the minority community in Pakistan and are stated to have sworn declarations renouncing their Pakistani nationality. It is also stated in the MEA's letter no. F6(44)/57-PSP, dated the 14.4.58 that in most of these cases their permanent settlement in India would eventually be granted. Their present ineligibility for registration under section 5(1) (a) of the C.Act is therefore *only technical* ... in cases where the applicants belonging to the minority community in Pakistan are staying on in India swearing affidavits that they have surrendered/lost their Pakistani

passports, it was for the authorities to satisfy themselves that the intention was to permit the persons
concerned to stay on indefinitely in India or the
applicants have severed all connections with Pakistan
and intend to settle down permanently in India; and
in cases where the authorities are so satisfied, the
applicants can be registered under section 5(1)(a).....[1]

Apart from the legal absorption of displaced persons
as enfranchised citizens, laws were being framed to
transform the displaced into productive citizens. The
Bihar government, for example, sought permission from
the central government to promulgate an Ordinance—
the Bihar Displaced Persons Rehabilitation (Acquisition
of Land) Ordinance—'to provide for the speedy acquisition of land for the rehabilitation of displaced persons
from Pakistan'.[2] The statement of objects and reasons
of the bill subsequently introduced, explained that an
extraordinary legal measure was required to fulfil the

[1] Note dated 18 July 1958, Ministry of Home Affairs
(Indian Citizenship Section). File no. 10/1/56, MHA–IC,
NAI (emphasis added).

[2] Note of the PRO, Ministry of Agriculture, dated 23
August 1950. File no. 17/143/50 MHA–Judl, NAI.

commitment of the state government to 'receive and rehabilitate 50,000 displaced persons from Eastern Pakistan', about 50 per cent of whom were agriculturalists. The bill provided for the 'speedy acquisition of waste and fallow lands' for the rehabilitation of different classes of displaced persons, and for acquiring wastelands in rural areas for 'the rehabilitation of the agriculturalists amongst the displaced persons' using their 'special experience' in the cultivation of jute for promoting jute productions in Purnea and Saharsa. The debates that ensued during the passage of the bill in the Bihar Legislative Assembly and the Legislative Council show a strong concern towards converting the doles on maintaining the refugees in camps, from unproductive to productive expenditure. By using their special skills to enhance jute production in the state, the refugees could be transformed into assets, from their present status of liability. The bill received presidential assent on 8 November 1950.

Several years after partition, the question of citizenship of 'displaced persons' continues to be entangled in legal indeterminacy. Following the amendments in the Citizenship Act of India in 1986 and 2003, large groups of people who had migrated from Pakistan across both the western and eastern borders have come to occupy the ambiguous space of being either 'illegal' migrants and, therefore, suspect aliens, or stateless 'nowhere' people without legal claims to citizenship. Two judgements coming after the 1986 amendment have, however, laid down principles that open up the closures in the legal regime of citizenship in India.

One of these judgements came in the context of the legal conundrum over the citizenship of Chakma refugees in India. Chakmas are Buddhists who fled to India from the Chittagong Hill Tracts and Mymensingh district of East Pakistan in 1964, displaced by the Kaptai Hydel Power Project. They sought refuge in Assam and Tripura and became Indian citizens in due course. Since Assam experienced the largest influx, it requested other states to share the responsibility. About 57 families comprising 4,012 Chakmas were settled in parts of Arunachal Pradesh (then NEFA or North East Frontier Agency), and allotted land in consultation with the local tribals. The decision to settle the Chakmas in Arunachal Pradesh was taken as an exceptional measure, since Arunachal Pradesh enjoys a special status in the federal arrangements in India, which disallows outsiders from owning property/land in the

121

state. Seen initially as temporary residents, the cumulative inflow and continued presence of the Chakmas in the state, generated anxiety among the indigenous Arunachalis around the social, economic, and cultural implications of their stay. The AAPSU (All Arunachal Pradesh Students Union) led the struggle to oust the Chakmas from the state. They resorted to social and economic boycott, coercion, discrimination as well as appeals to the central government to find a long-term solution.

The family of Khudiram Chakma was one among the 57 families of Chakma refugees that migrated to India in 1964. Lodged initially in the Government Refugee Camp at Ledo in Assam, they were later shifted to another camp at Miao in Arunachal Pradesh. In 1966, the state government drew up the Chakma Resettlement Scheme for refugees and allotted them land in two villages in Arunachal Pradesh. Khudiram Chakma and the other Chakma families left the allotment, and settled on land acquired through private negotiations in an area designated 'protected' under the Foreigners' (Protected Area) Order 1958. The local inhabitants complained against the encroachment of land by the Chakmas and accused them of other illegal activities including association with extremist groups. The state government instituted an inquiry into the legality of the land transaction, and in 1984 directed the Chakma families to shift back to the area set aside for them. After the amendment to the Citizenship Act in 1986, Khudiram Chakma invoked the newly inserted Section 6A, which laid down that all those who arrived in Assam before 1966 were citizens of India, to challenge the state government's order. Khudiram Chakma argued before the Guwahati High Court that the Chakmas settled in Arunachal Pradesh were citizens of India and their forcible eviction by the state government was a violation of their fundamental rights. The high court, however, held that the Chakmas did not fall in the category covered by Section 6A, 'as they had stayed in Assam for only a short period in 1964, and had *strayed away there from* in the area now within the State of Arunachal Pradesh' (emphasis added). They could not, therefore, be construed as being ordinarily the residents of Assam. The decision of the high court was upheld by the Supreme Court in *State of Arunachal Pradesh* v. *Khudiram Chakma*.[3]

[3] 1994 AIR 1461 (hereinafter referred to as *Khudiram Chakma*).

In a landmark judgement in January 1996, in the case of *National Human Rights Commission* v. *State of Arunachal Pradesh and Another*,[4] the Supreme Court revisited its judgement in the *Khudiram Chakma* case. Distinguishing the legal–procedural dimensions of citizenship raised in the *Khudiram Chakma* case (confined to Section 6A arising out of the Assam Accord) from the substantive issues of rights and justice that were raised by the National Human Rights Commission (NHRC), the Supreme Court brought the Chakmas within the purview of Section 5(1)(a) of the Citizenship Act, which provides for citizenship by registration. Having been resettled in the state of Arunachal Pradesh for more than three decades (at the time of making the petition), the Chakmas reminded the Government of India of the periodical guarantees of citizenship that had been given to them by the government. A public statement of such an assurance was first made in a joint declaration by the governments of India and Bangladesh in New Delhi in February 1972, with the central government conveying its decision to all the states to

[4] 1996 AIR 1234 (hereinafter referred to as *National Human Rights Commission*).'

confer citizenship on the Chakmas in accordance with Section 5(1)(a) of the Act. Significantly, while the 1986 Amendment Act could not (as decided by the Supreme Court decision in the *Khudiram Chakma* case) provide the ground for conferring citizenship to the Chakmas, it also precluded citizenship by birth to their children born in India, unless of course, the Chakmas were conferred citizenship. While the immediate context precipitating the petition was the 'quit notices' served on 'foreigners' by the AAPSU, at the centre of the conflict was the question whether the Chakmas had *any* claim at all to Indian citizenship and to the right to residence in the state of Arunachal Pradesh. The resolution of the question involved the constitutional right of indigenous Arunachalis to preserve their culture, territory, and resources from outsiders, and a competing assertion by the Chakmas of their claims to citizenship as a human right.

The NHRC steered clear of this contest, by couching its appeal not as an issue of citizenship requiring legal resolution, but as a human rights concern embodied in the right to life guaranteed in the constitution to both citizens and aliens. The claim to citizenship in the petition was couched not merely in a desire for legal membership, but the protection which legal membership was to bring in its wake. Thus the petition made before the Supreme Court by the NHRC following the complaints it received from certain groups of Chakmas, the People's Union for Civil Liberties (PUCL) Delhi, and the Committee for the Citizenship Rights of Chakmas (CCRC), sought to enforce the fundamental right to life under Article 21 of the constitution of 'about 65,000 Chakma/Hajong tribals … *being persecuted by sections of the citizens of Arunachal Pradesh*'. The government of Arunachal Pradesh and the central government were made respondents in the case. The Supreme Court subsequently issued an interim order directing the state government to ensure that 'the Chakmas situated in its territory are not ousted by any coercive action, not in accordance with law'(emphasis added).

The position of the central government, as expressed in its response to the petition by the NHRC, emerged from two premises—(a) a reminder to the Arunachal Pradesh government of its commitment to the resettlement of the Chakmas, which was made in 1964 after a negotiated settlement between the state government and the central government, and the central

government's commitment to its international obligations emerging from negotiations with the government of Bangladesh; (b) the legal intricacies and
human rights concerns that the issue inadvertently
generated. The central government, moreover, alleged
that the state government had not been forwarding
to it the applications submitted by the Chakmas, as
required under Rule 9 of the Citizenship Rules, 1955.
It suggested to the court that it favoured a dialogue
between the state government, the Chakmas, and all
concerned parties within the state to amicably resolve
the issue of granting citizenship to the Chakmas
while also redressing the grievances of the citizens of
Arunachal Pradesh.

The Arunachal Pradesh government's response to
the petition by NHRC was also based on two premises, rejecting both, the commitment to citizenship for
the Chakmas that the central government demanded,
and the allegations of human rights violations that the
NHRC made. For the state government, the question of conferring citizenship on the Chakmas had
been conclusively determined and foreclosed by the
Supreme Court's decision in *Khudiram Chakma* case.
The Chakmas were not entitled to the fundamental

rights of citizens, except the right to life, which the state government contended was adequately protected. Drawing upon the special protected status of Arunachal Pradesh in the constitution, the state government asserted that the Chakmas were foreigners, and the state government was within its rights to ask them to quit the state. The state government further claimed to have followed the procedure laid down in the Citizenship Act of 1955 and Rules of 1956, whereby the local administration could exercise a considerable degree of discretion in deciding applications for citizenship. In the Arunachal Pradesh government's interpretation, the procedure involved an application to the District Collector (DC) of the area, who then made enquiries about the antecedents of the applicant. A *satisfactory* report would be forwarded to the state government, which in turn would forward it to the central government. If a person (a Chakma, in this case) received no response to an application for citizenship, the state government argued, it was not because the application was pending before the DC, but because it would have been disposed of after the enquiry found it to be unsatisfactory. Eventually, however, this basically meant that the applications were not forwarded to the central government and the applicants themselves were not informed of any action.

The Supreme Court refused to accept the contention made by the state government that there was no threat to the life and liberty of the Chakmas and that adequate steps had been taken to ensure their protection. It endorsed the findings of the NHRC and the position of the central government, concluding that there existed 'a clear and present danger to the lives and personal liberty of the Chakmas'. Elaborating on the relevant rules governing the procedure for obtaining citizenship, the Supreme Court made it clear that under Section 5(1)(a) of the act, an application could be made under the existing rules to the collector within whose jurisdiction the applicant was ordinarily resident. The collector was required to transmit every application received by him to the central government, along with a report on specific matters required under the different clauses of the section. The court found it objectionable that the local administration in Arunachal Pradesh had *thwarted the procedure* by 'rejecting the application at the threshold', failing in its duty and preventing the central government from performing its duty under the Citizenship Act and the

Rules. Subsequently, the court issued the following directions:

1. The government of Arunachal Pradesh was to ensure that the life and personal liberty of all Chakmas residing within the state was protected. The state government could requisition the services of paramilitary or police force, and could request the central government to provide additional force.

2. The Chakmas were not to be evicted from their homes and denied domestic life and comfort, except according to the procedures laid down in the law.

3. The quit notices and ultimatums issued by the AAPSU and any other group amounted to threats to the life and liberty of the Chakmas. The state government ought to deal with such groups according to law.

4. Any application made for registration as a citizen of India by the Chakmas under Section 5 of the Act, was to be entered in the register maintained for the purpose and forwarded to the

central government by the DC. The applications that had been returned were to be recalled or fresh ones obtained to be processed.

5. While the application of any individual Chakma was being considered, the state government could not evict or remove the person from his home or occupation on the grounds that he was not a citizen of India.

The claims to state protection by both the Chakmas and the Arunachalis generated distinct and competing idioms of citizenship. The Arunachalis drew on the promise the constitution made to them, assuring them the right to preserve their culture, territory, and resources, and protection against the erosion of these rights by outsiders. The Chakmas pressed a claim to protection of a different kind—the recognition of substantive membership as citizens—which went beyond what was afforded to them through subsumption under the category of a refugee under the care of the state. Unlike the Arunachalis who pressed the central government to secure to them the constitutional guarantees of differentiated citizenship, for the Chakmas it was only universal undifferentiated citizenship that could assure the erasure of their liminal status of being a 'nowhere people'.

The Passports Act, 1967 is the only law in India which recognizes statelessness as a condition for issuing a certificate of identity to refugees. Namgyal Dolkar, the daughter of Tibetan refugees born in Tibet and residing in Himachal Pradesh, sought to convert her status as a refugee into an Indian citizen by birth. Namgyal Dolkar was born on 13 April 1986, before the 1986 Citizenship Amendment Act came into effect. In 2005, Dolkar applied for an identity certificate, which she was made to understand could be surrendered if she wished to obtain an Indian passport. On 10 March 2008, she applied to the Delhi Regional Passport Office for an Indian passport, in which she mentioned that she was a citizen of India by birth and had never possessed any other citizenship. Her application was returned with the objection that she had suppressed the information that she possessed an identity certificate as a refugee and that her parents were Tibetan refugees, both of which made her ineligible for an Indian passport. Namgyal Dolkar petitioned the High Court of Delhi against the decision of the

Regional Passport Office in Delhi. The Ministry of
External Affairs (MEA), which was the respondent
in the case, made the arguments that the petitioner
was registered under the Foreigners Act as a Tibetan
national; under the Passport Act and Rules she could
possess only one travel document, and since she already
possessed an identity card which enabled her to travel,
she could not be issued a passport too. Moreover, the
MEA argued, under a policy decision taken by the
Ministry of Home Affairs, a Tibetan national who
entered India after March 1959 could not become an
Indian citizen by naturalization. A Tibetan national
could be considered, however, for citizenship under
Section 5(1)(c) of the Citizenship Act, if they married an Indian national. Justice S. Muralidhar of the
Delhi High Court rejected all the arguments of the
MEA. The concept of nationality, he argued, had no
legislative recognition in the Citizenship Act, and the
petitioner's description of herself as a Tibetan national
was of no legal consequence as far as the act was concerned. The fact that in the application form for an
identity certificate, the petitioner described herself as
a Tibetan national cannot, therefore, be construed as
'a waiver of the right to be recognised as an Indian

citizen by birth, a right that is expressly conferred by Section 3(1) of the Citizenship Act'. Such a statement could not be treated as renunciation of Indian citizenship, either. Moreover, he pointed out, a citizen by birth was entitled to a passport, and did not need to apply for citizenship.[5] Directing the Regional Passport Office to issue her an Indian passport, based on the ground that she was a citizen of India by birth, the judgement paved the ground for Namgyal Dolkar becoming the first Tibetan to be considered an Indian citizen by birth. More fundamentally, the court laid down the principles whereby statelessness could be prevented by facilitating the possession of citizenship.

The Displaced Person and the Security State

In its decision in the *National Human Rights Commission* and later in *Sarbanand Sonowal* v. *Union of India*[6] cases, the Supreme Court made the central government

[5] *Namgyal Dolkar* v. *Government of India, Ministry of External Affairs*, writ petition W.P. (C) 12179/2009, High Court of Delhi, decided on 22 December 2010.

[6] AIR 2005 SC 2920.

predominant in matters concerning citizenship. The premises of the decisions made in the two cases were, however, divergent. In the NHRC case, the Supreme Court lay down the procedural guidelines, which *enabled* the central government and also made it *responsible* for the protection of the rights of a people rendered stateless. In the Sarbanand Sonowal case, on the other hand, the court buttressed the sovereignty of the state, directing it to transform itself into a security state against the dangerous and disruptive presence of the illegal migrant, and giving it the *authority* to expel them. The Supreme Court judgement construed the migrant as an aggressor whose identification and expulsion was important for the protection of state sovereignty.

In the recent past, the contest over illegal migration and citizenship has played out in judicial pronouncements in two sets of public interest litigations (PILs). Both these sets of PILs manifest the following paradox that the NHRC and Sarbanand Sonowal judgements presented: that the exercise of state sovereignty is made manifest in complying with the universal frameworks of human rights; and on the other hand, state sovereignty is dependent upon the need to differentiate, exclude, and expel the non-citizens, a task considered

135

imperative to secure its territory and population. The PILs questioned the validity of Section 6A of the Citizenship Act. One of these, brought before the Supreme Court by the Assam Sanmilita Mahasangha (in *Assam Sanmilita Mahasangha and Others* v. *Union of India and Another,* 2014) focused specifically on the provision in section 6A granting Indian citizenship to those who entered Assam between 1966 and 1971. The second PIL filed by the Bimalanghsu Roy Foundation in 2012, on the other hand, which is still being heard, focused on the part of Section 6A that treats all migrants who entered Assam after 1971 as illegal. The first PIL raised anxiety over the dilution of the legal frameworks of citizenship, which they argued promoted indiscriminate influx, and put at risk the security of the state and people. The second PIL lamented the clubbing of all migrants who entered India after 1971 as illegal, and asked that a distinction be made between illegal migrants and displaced persons in Assam, who must be given the legal status of citizens. As the discussion below will show, both the PILs converged in their concern for buttressing the security apparatus of the government, to enable the sifting of desirable from undesirable persons. The second petition, in addition, sought a legal resolution of the predicament of displaced persons, which had been left to administrative discretion since Independence. The possibility of using this discretion was erased by the 1986 amendment to the Citizenship Act.

Between 2009 and 2014, a cluster of petitions filed by the NGOs Assam Sanmilita Mahasangha, Assam Public Works, and All Assam Ahom Association in the Supreme Court, challenged the validity of Sections 6A (3) and (4) of the Citizenship Act which provided that migrants from East Pakistan who entered Assam between January 1966 and March 1971 could become citizens of India. The court construed that the appeal from the NGOs represented the interests of an entire people—the tribal and non-tribal population of the state of Assam—and therefore deserved to be admitted. These interests, the judges observed, related to the protection of the Assamese culture, but also had ramifications for the sovereignty and integrity of the country as a whole:

> In their petition, they have raised a plea that the sovereignty and integrity of India is itself at stake as a massive influx of illegal migrants from a neighboring country has affected this core Constitutional value.

That, in fact, it has been held in Sonowal's case that
such an influx is 'external aggression' within the
meaning of Article 355 of the Constitution of India,
and that the Central Government has done precious
little to stem this tide thereby resulting in a violation
of Article 355.... Not only is there an assault on the
life of the citizenry of the State of Assam but there is
an assault on their way of life as well. The culture of
an entire people is being eroded in such a way that
they will ultimately be swamped by persons who have
no right to continue to live in this country. The petitioners have also argued that this Hon'ble Court in
Sonowal's case has specifically held in para 79 thereof
that Bangladeshi nationals who have illegally crossed
the border and have trespassed into Assam or are living
in other parts of the country have no legal right of any
kind to remain in India and are liable to be deported.
They have also raised a fervent plea that Article 14
also continues to be violated as Section 6A (3) to (5)
are not time bound but are ongoing. (*Assam Sanmilita
Mahasangha and Others* v. *Union of India and Another*,
W. P. (Civil) no. 562 of 2012, Supreme Court of India,
decided on 17 December 2014)

The judges, however, left the question pertaining to
the constitutional validity of Section 6A to be addressed

by an appropriate bench of a minimum of five judges, since it involved substantial questions involving the interpretation of constitutional provisions. A fundamental question pertained to the compatibility of Section 6A with the citizenship provisions in Part II of the constitution, since the Citizenship Act in 1986 had prescribed a cut-off date for citizenship in Assam (March 1971), which was different from the cut-off dates set by Article 6 of the constitution (1 March 1947 and 19 July 1948) for the consideration of people crossing the borders between India and Pakistan. In addition, the judges queried, whether by diluting the political and cultural rights of the people of Assam, Section 6A conflicted with the following fundamental and legal rights conferred by the constitution: (i) the right against discrimination and universal adult suffrage in Articles 325 and 326 of the constitution; (ii) the fundamental right to conservation of culture in Article 29(1) of the constitution; (iii) the right of people to be protected against external aggression and internal disturbance implied in Article 355 of the constitution; (v) the right against discrimination in Article 14 by marking out Assam from other border states to apply the special provisions of Section 6A; (vi) right to life and personal liberty in Article 21 of the constitution since the lives of the Assamese people were affected by the massive influx of illegal migrants from Bangladesh.

While entrusting the above questions to the scrutiny of a constitutional bench, the judges ventured to address the remaining parts of the petition concerning Section 6A. Tracing the historical context of Section 6A to the Assam Accord, the judges averred that the legal modalities of identification and conferment of citizenship were only one part of the Assam Accord. The other and equally substantial components of the accord consisted in securing the international border against future infiltration and the preservation of Assamese culture and identity. According to clause 6 of the Assam Accord, 'constitutional, legislative and administrative safeguards' were to be provided 'to protect, preserve and promote the cultural, social, linguistic identity and heritage of the Assamese people'. In October 2006, the government of Assam constituted a Committee of Ministers to examine all the issues relating to the implementation of clause 6 of the Assam Accord, and the complex task of defining the 'Assamese people'. The committee met with political parties, literary bodies, and student groups to deliberate on an appropriate definition. In July 2011, a cabinet subcommittee was constituted by the central government to examine the question.

Leaving it to the two governments and the Assamese people to deliberate and decide on what constituted Assamese culture, the Supreme Court limited itself to issuing specific directions to the central and state governments for the fortification of the eastern border, through fencing, building roads to facilitate patrolling, putting up floodlights along the border, effective vigil along the riverine boundary, and so on. The court, moreover, decided to monitor the government's progress and prepare a roadmap for the completion of the process. It was, however, not only the strengthening of the border which the court contemplated, it also gave attention to securing the territory 'internally' by expediting the process of sieving out foreigners from citizens. To this end, it asked the Guwahati High Court to hasten the process of the selection of chairpersons and members of the Foreigners Tribunals to ensure that they became operational. The Chief Justice of the Guwahati High Court was asked to monitor the functioning of the tribunals by constituting a Special Bench, which would sit at least once every month to oversee their progress. The central government was asked to streamline the process of deportation of the declared illegal migrants after discussions with the government of Bangladesh, and to place the outcome of these discussions before the court. In addition, the Supreme Court laid down a time schedule to be followed for updating the National Register of Citizens (NRC) in Assam so that the entire register could be published by the end of January 2016.[7] In its administrative guidelines the Supreme Court appears to have acted in line with its decision in *Sarbanand Sonowal* in construing the 'influx of illegal migrants into the state of India as external aggression'. At the same time, however, it broadens the notion of security to include 'internal disturbance', which involved being

[7] Judgement delivered by Justices Ranjan Gogoi and R.F. Nariman on 17 December 2014 in the case *Assam Sanmilita Mahasangha and Others* v. *Union of India and Others* [Writ Petition (Civil) No. 562 of 2012]. In May 2015, the Supreme Court appointed a court commissioner to visit the border areas to study and report the progress to court. The judges pulled up the central and state governments for not doing enough to buttress the eastern border, which posed a security risk to the lives of ordinary citizens.

alert to and eliminating risks to the Assamese people from outsiders. To this end, it directed the attention of the larger bench of the Supreme Court which would examine the constitutional questions precipitated by the petitions, to consider whether the expression 'state' occurring in Article 355, refers only to a territorial region or includes also the people living in the state, their culture and identity. For its part, by prescribing a deadline for the update of the NRC, the court reinforced the responsibility taken up by the central government through the Assam Accord to update the 1951 NRC in Assam.

While the update of the NRC is being carried out in Assam under the supervision of the Supreme Court, both the process of the update and the debate over the definition of 'an Assamese' have generated contests in Assam. For a section of the Assamese people—in particular Muslims of Bengali origin in Assam—the process holds the promise of bringing a closure to the burden of suspect citizenship they have carried. On the other hand, the quest towards defining an Assamese identity shows a tendency of slipping towards an ethno-religious assertion, which could roll back the civic foundations of the NRC.

The second set of petitions is still being heard by the Supreme Court and pertains to the citizenship of displaced Hindu migrants from Bangladesh. Filed in 2012 by two NGOs, Swajan and the Bimalangshu Roy Foundation, the petitioners pleaded that Hindus and persons belonging to other minority communities migrating from Bangladesh to Assam to escape religious persecution must not be bracketed with illegal migrants to be slotted for deportation. According to the Assam Accord, and the subsequent amendment to the Citizenship Act, all persons who crossed over from Bangladesh after 1971 are illegal migrants and must be deported. The petitioners pointed out that Section 2 of the Immigrants (Expulsion from Assam) Act, 1950 protects from expulsion any person 'who on account of civil disturbances or fear of such disturbances' in any area forming part of Pakistan (now Bangladesh), 'has been displaced from or has left his place of residence and has been subsequently residing in Assam'. The petitioners asked that displaced persons should constitute a distinct category for legal protection from deportation. Observing that the problem of religious minorities coming from Bangladesh to India was not confined to Assam, in July 2013, the Supreme Court extended the case to the entire country, making 18 state governments party to it. This is a significant move on the part of the Supreme Court since it lends weight to the petitioner's argument that the Hindus seeking shelter in Assam should be given citizenship on the same grounds that they have been given in Gujarat and Rajasthan between 2004 and 2007 (*The Telegraph* 2013). If in the *Assam Sanmilita* petition the focus was on the provision of Section 6A of the Citizenship Act which provided for citizenship for those who had migrated to India between 1966 and 1971, the present case put under scrutiny the part of Section 6A which applied to those who had migrated into Assam after 1971, and were to be deported as illegal migrants. If the former expressed anxiety at the inadequate buttressing of Assamese borders and people against the influx from across the eastern borders, the latter was critical of the erasure that was made of the distinctiveness of displaced persons who were victims of civil disturbance (in the form of religious persecution), which was available in the Immigrants (Expulsion from Assam) Act, 1950. These displaced persons, the petitioners pleaded, should not be clubbed with illegal migrants, and given the status of refugees under the international conventions or citizenship.

Treading carefully on the question of granting citizenship on the basis of religion, the UPA government in the centre did not file any official response to the petition (Sriram 2015). After the NDA came to power in 2014, its leaders, including the BJP chief Amit Shah spoke in rallies in Assam assuring citizenship to Hindus who had fled to India to escape religious persecution in Bangladesh. At the same time, echoing the campaign speeches of Prime Minister Narendra Modi in the Lok Sabha election, Amit Shah said the BJP would get rid of illegal immigrants or 'infiltrators' (Sriram 2015). The BJP has declared that immigration policy will be a major plank on which it will contest the Assam Assembly elections in 2016. In the meantime, the government has issued a statement that it is likely to enact a law for the rehabilitation of Hindu refugees from Pakistan and Bangladesh.[8]

[8] A task force was set up to expedite pending citizenship requests from refugees and issuing long-term visas extending up to 10 to 15 years wherever the citizenship requests were taking long to process.

Fragmented Citizenship: Citizens Enclaved

Enclaves are pockets of territory on which a particular nation state has sovereign jurisdiction, but are located in and surrounded by the territory of another nation state. Till the summer of 2015, when an understanding between the Indian and Bangladeshi governments was reached, Indian enclaves were Indian territories within the territorial boundaries of Bangladesh. Similar Bangladeshi enclaves existed inside Indian territory. Residents of such enclaves were citizens of the country to which the enclave belonged, but governmental machinery had meagre or no access to the enclaves, since its legal–juridical sovereignty over the enclaves was interrupted by and subject to the territorial sovereignty of another state. Enclaved citizens did not reside within the contiguous nation state boundary of India. Unlike displaced persons they had not migrated into India to stake claims to future rights of residence and citizenship. But for all practical purposes they were displaced persons with ambivalent citizenship, since they were denied political rights and constitutional protections, and led a precarious life of perpetual liminality.

Also called chitmahals, the enclaves were for long implicated in the border disputes between India and Bangladesh. A product of the manner in which the boundaries were drawn in straight lines along areas where land was intersected by a web of water bodies on the eastern borders, and a peculiar legacy of state accession, the Indian and Bangladeshi enclaves were the successor territories of land belonging to the Raja of Cooch Behar and the Mughal Faujdar of Rangpur, who acceded to India and Pakistan respectively. As a result of this, a situation arose where islands of alien-jurisdiction were created in the sovereign territory of another state. According to a survey carried out by the Indian and Bangladeshi governments in April 1997, 111 Indian enclaves existed in Bangladesh and 51 Bangladeshi enclaves existed in India along the eastern borders in the states of Assam, West Bengal, Meghalaya, and Tripura. There were among these, counter-enclaves and counter-counter-enclaves, which were fragments of Bangladeshi territory surrounded by Indian territory, which in turn, was surrounded by Bangladeshi territory.

The contest over enclaves played out in a way where political anxieties veered between holding on to land as territory over which the nation has exclusive proprietary control, to the other end, of abandoning land to ensure the integrity of national territorial borders. At both these ends lay the concern over the dissociation between cartography and territory and the dilution of state sovereignty because of territorial fragmentation. These concerns played out at different points of time in the relationship between India and Pakistan (later Bangladesh). Citizenship correspondingly vacillated between its association with territory as the source of national and political identity, and on the other hand, territory becoming aligned with livelihood practices and lifeworld. In its association with livelihood, territory invoked a sense of belonging to the geographically contiguous area of the other nation state, which then became a source of effective identity, substituting the physically distant mother country as the source of affective belonging and political identity of citizenship. Between the two, the people residing in the enclaves have experienced fragmented citizenship, where the quest for belonging has led to their aporetic existence, alternating between illegality, displacement, and notional legal citizenship. For permission to leave the enclave and enter Bangladeshi territory, a resident of an Indian enclave needed a passport and visa issued from mainland India—and that required crossing Bangladeshi territory. As a newspaper reported: 'Indian citizens in Bangladesh are often forced to provide false information to Bangladeshi officials to conduct business, send their children to school or receive medical care nearby, said Mizanur Rahman, a 34-year-old farmer from Dashiar Chara and a father of two. Duplicity is at the core of an enclave-dweller's existence, he said' (IRIN 2011).

The history of this contestation traversed two distinct phases, with the creation of Bangladesh in 1971 as the point of demarcation. The first phase was marked by the Nehru-Noon agreement over the 'disputed' territory of the Berubari Union and the exchange of enclaves, and the Supreme Court decision turning it down. Berubari Union No. 12 was an area of 8.75 square miles in the Jalpaiguri district. The dispute over Berubari Union arose because of the discrepancy in the award made by the Radcliffe Commission entrusted with the responsibility of demarcating the boundary between the two newly created provinces of West and East Bengal. In the narrative text of the award, the Commission described Berubari Union as part of

West Bengal. But the map annexed to the narrative text, showed it as part of East Bengal. In 1958, the governments of India and Pakistan signed an agreement to resolve boundary disputes. According to the Nehru-Noon agreement, as it was called, the government of India would cede the southern part of the Berubari Union to East Pakistan and exchange all the enclaves created by the Radcliffe Line, whereby both the countries would acquire the enclaves located in their territory. The agreement thus sought to assuage cartographic anxieties of the newly created nation states and ensure the correspondence between territorial borders and territorial sovereignty. The agreement precipitated outrage in West Bengal and elsewhere over what was seen as loss of territory for India, and compelled the President of India to seek a reference from the Supreme Court to ascertain the constitutional validity of the agreement. On 14 March 1960, an eight-member bench of the Supreme Court decided that the agreement did not amount to a mere determination of boundaries, which was within the purview of the powers of the government, but involved cessation or alienation of a part of India's territory. The power to cede territory, the judges concluded, rested only with the Parliament and could become effective only through a constitutional amendment, which required political consensus. The Constitution (9th Amendment) Act (December 1960) was subsequently passed to amend the First Schedule of the constitution to give effect to the transfer of territories.

The legal wrangles and political turmoil that followed prevented immediate transfer. It was ultimately in 1974, following the creation of Bangladesh in 1971, that an accord was signed between the prime ministers of the two countries, Indira Gandhi and Mujib-ur-Rehman. The two countries agreed that Berubari would remain with India in exchange for the Bangladeshi enclave of Dahagram and Angarpota, with access to a tract of land, the Tinbigha Corridor, providing the link to mainland Bangladesh. The accord also repeated the earlier agreement on the exchange of all enclaves, with ramifications for the states of Assam, West Bengal, Meghalaya, and Tripura, in which the enclaves existed. The agreement remained unimplemented, however.

The Constitution 119th Amendment Act of 2015 sought to give closure to the longstanding dispute. Amidst the long-drawn process of settlement of the dispute over territory, the effectively stateless residents of the enclaves had for an equally long period remained in a state of ambivalent citizenship. In 2011, when then Indian Prime Minister Manmohan Singh visited Bangladesh to sign a protocol, the residents of Indian enclaves kept their homes in darkness to press their demand for Bangladeshi citizenship, which would entitle them to welfare programmes and employment opportunities. One such resident of an Indian enclave, Biplob Hossain, whose father had fought for Bangladesh's liberation in 1971, was an Indian citizen in an enclave inside Bangladesh. The exchange of enclaves, Hossain believed, would allow him to spend his remaining days as a Bangladeshi citizen. Hossain lived in Garholjorha-2 enclave, also known as Elengbarhi enclave, in Kurhigram with his wife and three children (Niloy 2015).

The Land Border Agreement Treaty signed between India and Bangladesh in June 2015 promised that the exchange of enclaves would not involve a displacement of population and that the territories of the enclaves would be absorbed by the two countries along with their residents, who would henceforth become legal citizens of the country of absorption. The residents of the enclave were also assured that they could exercise choice in citizenship. The question how those who left their enclaves of residence after its exchange and absorption, choosing the citizenship of the country to which the enclave originally belonged, would be rehabilitated as citizens, remains contentious. The historical processes of the removal of 'border anomalies' is yet another illustration of the association between national cartographies and citizenship. While legal citizenship conveys a notion of passive citizenship, where citizens desire legal inclusion, for those who are ambivalent citizens, legal citizenship is worth aspiring to. Citizenship then sustains as a condition of expanding horizons, and involves churnings that open up other possibilities of becoming citizens.

4

Becoming Citizens

Where is the tent?

Over there.

Draupadi fixes her red eyes on the tent. Says, Come, I'll go.

The guard pushes the water pot forward. Draupadi stands up. She pours the water down on the ground. Tears her piece of cloth with her teeth. Seeing such strange behavior, the guard says, She's gone crazy, and runs for orders.

... Senanayak walks out surprised and sees Draupadi, naked, walking toward him in the bright sunlight with her head high. The nervous guards trail behind.

... Draupadi wipes the blood on her palm and says in a voice that is as terrifying, sky splitting, and sharp as her ululation, What's the use of clothes? You can strip me, but how can you clothe me again? Are you a man?

... She looks around and chooses the front of Senanayak's white bush shirt to spit a bloody gob at and says, there isn't a man here that I should be ashamed. I will not let you put my cloth on me. What more can you do? Come on, *counter* me—come on, *counter* me—?

Draupadi pushes Senanayak with her two mangled breasts, and for the first time Senanayak is afraid to stand before an unarmed *target*, terribly afraid. (Spivak 1981)

Citizenship produces contested imaginaries of the political community and competing notions of the citizen and his/her terms of membership. Often citizenship is put forth as a momentum concept, foregrounding its integrative and universalizing aspects. Yet, the fact that citizenship is deeply contested, is experienced, and unfolds in specific social fields amidst heterogeneous and often contesting political imaginaries, assumptions, and practices, has also become influential in thinking about citizenship. Increasingly also, citizenship is no longer seen as embodying a politics of passive indifference, but as a condition replete with possibilities and the promise of radical change. Correspondingly, the social and political field that citizenship has come to traverse is no longer benign and impersonal. Rather, it signifies a continually reconfiguring field of contest. More often than not, the contest is over definitions and the corresponding limits they put on who belongs, how, and on what terms. From the articulation of cities as new arenas of graded entitlements, to citizenship practices which aim concertedly at the retrieval of the political as an interactive public space to congeal collective energies into shared bonds of citizenship, the landscapes of 'new citizenship' have arrayed themselves as a spectrum.

The legal enframing of the citizen involves a simultaneous production of its other, that is, the non-citizen. The non-citizen comprises a range of residual categories—the alien, the enemy alien, the migrant, the refugee, the illegal migrant, and so forth,—suggesting lifeworlds that cannot be captured in the legal enunciation of the citizen. If the non-citizen is the shadow of the citizen, inextricably linked to it, but unable to become the citizen, the world of citizens is also tumultuous, where the promise of equality collides with the requirement of privileged dissociation. Citizenship is therefore made up of multiple margins, which constitute the sites of constant churnings, releasing powerful new idioms, imaginaries, and practices of citizenship. It is at these margins of citizenship that the unintelligibility and opacity of citizenship is broken down, to produce moments and manoeuvres of transformative citizenship.

The figure of the citizen in postcolonial India embodied the contradictions of the transformative moment, which held out the promise of rupture from a past marked by deep social divisions and inequality. Yet the citizen remained sutured to the past by the dominant logic of the nation state and the exercise of social and political power, which are integral to the modern state. This contradiction has continued to manifest itself in the increasing association of citizenship with descent and blood ties and a quickening of the process of creation of residual citizens who are pushed to the margins, but ironically, refuse to recede or be contained by it. These citizens generate polyrhythms of citizenships, expressed in specific idioms of constitutional insurgency and insurgent citizenship. Citizenship may, therefore, be best understood both within and outside the narratives of law, in the force of the constituent power, which constantly pushes at the borders of citizenship. Negri's powerful imagery in terms of the 'massive' and exceptional force of the movement of constituent power, which has as its 'fundamental element' the 'continual creation of a new world of life', is useful for comprehending this (Negri cited in Baxi 2008).

Where and how do we identify these manifestations of transformative citizenship in contemporary time? How do the margins become a powerful indictment of the dominant vocabulary of citizenship? In a strident criticism of the processes by which the decline of the public sphere of politics takes place, Hannah Arendt (1958) locates its source in the emergence of the bureaucratic state, characterized by the 'rule by nobody', and an equally anonymous realm of the 'social'. Characterized by the predominance of economic contractual relationships, the realm of the social compels conformity, is grounded in a notion of 'mass society' that discourages the articulation of difference by enforcing norms of conduct, and eliminates and annihilates differences of culture, ideology, and the like. For Arendt, it was the public sphere, which she described as the sphere of appearance, distinguished by the presence of freedom and equality, where individuals as citizens interacted through the medium of speech and persuasion, disclosing thereby their unique identities, and decided through collective deliberation about matters of common concern. It was the world of appearance and its continual recreation that was for Arendt the only repository and guarantee of equality. The political community, referring to a group of people who come together and are bound by shared citizenship regardless of their culture, ethnic, and other loyalties, is the best possible form of the public sphere (Arendt 1958). Is it possible to identify such spaces of deliberation in the contemporary transformations in citizenship? What forms do such 'public worlds of appearance' take, and what is their impact, if any, on the entrenched hierarchies of citizenship?

Popular Sovereignty and Democratic Iterations

Partha Chatterjee makes a distinction between two modes in which citizenship practices have become part of the experiences of most of the postcolonial world. Making an analytical distinction between popular sovereignty and governmentality, and the corresponding categories of citizens and populations,

Chatterjee (2004) argues that the concept of the citizen is linked to the principle of popular sovereignty which holds that the legitimacy of the state and political power stems from the will of the people. Population, on the other hand, is linked to the principle of state legitimacy, which is constructed through policies that aim at providing services to the people, who are in turn made subject to the rationality and techniques of governing through the bureaucratic regimes of the developmental state. This conceptual distinction corresponds to specific modes of citizenship practices, one which is to be found in the domain of civil society, which is the realm of formal institutions and practices of dissociated rights bearing individuals and their associations, and their interactions with the formal structures of the state, constitution, and laws. Chatterjee proposes the idea of political society as encompassing the relationship between the developmental bureaucratic state and population groups, which are different from those that exist in civil society. While citizenship practices as they inform civil society are construed as the ideal, they remain confined to a demographically limited section of the people; the majority is 'only tenuously and even then ambiguously and contextually rights bearing citizen in the sense imagined by the constitution' (Chatterjee 2004: 38). Veena Das would, however, disagree with what she perceives as the binary posed by Chatterjee between the practices of citizenship in civil society and the politics of the governed in political society, which primarily consists of securing the goods 'necessary to preserve biological life' (Das 2011: 320). Through a study of the urban poor in an industrial periphery of the National Capital Region, Das shows that what are presented by Chatterjee as distinct and dual domains of political and biological life in effect 'bleed into each other' and through a process of 'mutual absorption' produce the capacity for the poor to lay claims to citizenship through a politics of 'haq' (Das 2011: 320). The rallying around 'haq' for the inhabitants of a shanty in NOIDA, makes it possible for the poor to assert citizenship as a moral claim rather than a status with entitlements, giving way to 'traces of law' in spaces that are not recognized as legal or juridical (Das 2011: 324).

People's practices of citizenship show, however, that the civil and the political cannot be two distinct domains occupied by citizens of different kinds, who express and achieve citizenship in mutually discrete

modes in disparate domains. Indeed, the narratives of
citizenship from the margins reveal that those who as
'population' groups are made subjects of the government's policies may actually straddle the domains of
both civil and political societies, making the boundaries between them permeable. Studies of people's
practices of citizenship in urban spaces have identified plural idioms of citizenship, and explained them
through concepts such as, the 'politics of the governed'
(Chatterjee 2004), 'insurgent citizenship' (Holston
2007), and the 'global street' (Sassen 2011). In these
studies the politics of the marginalized has been seen
as 'making room for manoeuvre' (Gordon and Stack
2007) to open up spaces from which the state may
be addressed for claims to citizenship. T.H. Marshall's
(1950) essay on citizenship and social class had shown
that the civil, political, and social aspects of citizenship, in the course of their development alongside
the economic impulses emerging from capitalism,
become dependent on the capitalist state for authoriz-
ing their rights. James Holston (2007) looks at cities,
which in the context of global urbanization, become
volatile, crowded with citizens and non-citizens, who
contest their exclusions. In such a context of volatility,

Holston argues 'citizenship is unsettled and unsettling' (Holston 2007: 3). It is the experiences of citizenship in these peripheries, particularly the 'hardships of illegal residence, house building, and land conflict', which become both the 'context and substance of a new urban citizenship' (Holston 2007: 3). The 'global city' (Sassen 1991) and the 'megacity' (Ong 2007) are important nodes in the global network of capital, which provide customized packages of citizenship. Citizenship is made attractive for those individuals whose skills and talents are considered valuable and who can, therefore, negotiate their terms of belonging. These are mobile citizens, who maximize their gains and opportunities through flexibility of movement, rather than rigidity with stability of location. While paving the way for flexible and entrepreneurial citizenship, the megacity is also the space where the presence of citizenship-like rights does not necessarily require deeper bonds of belonging. Indeed, the global megacity is a space of 'graduated sovereignties' (Ong 2007), where entrepreneurial expatriates claim the rights and benefits which hitherto belonged exclusively to citizens, and on the other hand the space of stable (as distinct from mobile/flexible) citizenship is fraught with hierarchized ordering of citizens. The vast masses of the labouring poor, who are seen as adding no value to the city beyond their bare existence, make for the zoning of cities into graded pockets of entitlements and deprivations. Yet, cities are also seen as sources of human rights, for opening up new arenas of political claims by ordinary people to justice and account-ability from the state, and guarantees of democratic freedoms (Ong 2006: 502). James Holston's study of difference-based citizenship in Brazil and insurgent citizenship movements in the urban peripheries is reflective of how the labouring poor and the work-ing class can transform both the idioms and authorship of citizenship.

Saskia Sassen (2003) and Aihwa Ong (2006) see the urban streets and the cyber world as spaces of citizen-ship formation and performance, where diverse groups may come together as epistemic communities to pro-test against the state and demand an end to corruption, nepotism, and autocratic rule. Differing from Hardt and Negri's (2005), conception of the multitude as the revolutionary subject which resists the ubiquitous penetration of global capital, Seyla Benhabib (2007) stresses the need for a different kind of resistance, which takes on institutional structures of domination to produce and reinforce popular sovereignty. Distancing herself from the metaphors of 'networking', 'entanglement', 'spread of communicative forms', and the like, which have been used in their analysis by Ong and others, Benhabib emphasizes that these forms of action present a world without institutional actors and without structured centres and sites of resistance. Hardt and Negri's revolutionary subject, the multitude, Benhabib argues, is not the Citizen, since it is not the carrier of popular sovereignty, and lacks the drive toward the constitutionalization of power. Benhabib (2007: 14) makes a case for a politics of democratic iterations, referring to complex processes of public deliberations that take place in institutions of the state and civil society. The sites at which democratic iterations can take place are the entrenched and structured political and representative public institutions like the legislatures, decision-making bodies like the executive and the judiciary, as well as in what Benhabib calls the 'informal' and 'weak' publics of civil society associations and the media. If for Benhabib, the enhancement of democratic citizenship takes place in institutionalized spaces, for Sassen (2011), it is in the urban spaces that a non-ritualized public space of appearance erupts through the 'production of "presence" by those without power'. Going beyond what she calls the 'empirics of specific cases' (for example, Tahrir Square in Cairo, Sana'a in Yemen, protests in Tel Aviv among a string of other urban protests worldwide), Sassen conceptualizes the 'global street' as the public space of action in the city. Different from the spaces of ritualized protest, the urban street becomes the site where larger social and economic transformations and conflicts, both urban and rural, make themselves manifest. Both these forms— Benhabib's framework of democratic iterations, which augment popular sovereignty, and Sassen's global street as the space for the performance of a universal event of protest—contribute to an understanding of the diverse modes through which the powerless can make history.

Citizen intervention in the institutional domain of the state has often been an important mode for the articulation of a democratic public space. Indeed, both the judiciary and the legislature have provided spaces for citizen activism. Integrally located in the ruling apparatus of the state, as lawmaking and adjudicating institutions, the Supreme Court and the Parliament have often also become sites where the elaboration of citizenship has taken place through insurgent citizenship practices. With the emergence of social action litigation, in particular, the Supreme Court has participated in governance and policymaking, often becoming a conduit for political engagements between the state and the people. On the other hand, as a referee institution, it has widened the scope of political rights (in particular the right to political participation and the freedom of speech and expression) in the electoral domain, and regulated the relative powers of political and statutory institutions.

Judicial pronouncements have brought into prominence issues of citizens' trust in political and public institutions. These have been particularly prominent in cases brought by citizens' groups for the scrutiny of the court. One such case pertaining to electoral reforms focused on transparency and criminalization of politics culminating in the citizens' right to know. In May 2002, and subsequently in March 2003, civil society groups—the Association for Democratic Reforms, Lok Satta, and People's Union for Civil Liberties—brought a public interest litigation before the Supreme Court asking for the implementation of the Law Commission's recommendation that the details pertaining to the background of candidates contesting an election must be made public. In its judgement, the Supreme Court enhanced the powers of the Election Commission of India and the rights of the citizen–voter. Envisaging Article 324 of the constitution, as a 'reservoir of powers', the court gave the Election Commission 'residuary powers', 'where law [was] silent', empowering it to step in to fill any legal vacuum in the conduct of elections, till a suitable law was enacted.[1] The court simultaneously made the submission of affidavits by candidates contesting elections, giving details of their backgrounds (criminal cases, if any, and economic assets), compulsory. Underlying the judgement was the principle that the courts were ultimately addressing the fundamental rights of the people and the principles of democratic participation. Democracy, the judges asserted, could not survive 'without free and fair elections, without free and fairly informed voters'. Votes cast by 'uninformed voters' would be meaningless. The significance of the judgement, therefore, lay in the

[1] *Union of India* v. *Association for Democratic Reforms & Anr* (2002) SC 249 (hereinafter referred to as *Association for Democratic Reforms*).

enhancement of the scope of the fundamental right of citizens to the freedom of speech and expression (Article 19[1]). The 'casting of votes ... that is to say, the voter speaks out ... by casting the vote', as a form of 'speech and expression' required as any fundamental rights, the conditions conducive for its exercise. Conducive conditions would cover not only conditions which allowed the voter merely to cast the vote, but also conditions in which the act of voting would be meaningful and fulfilling for both the voter and for the political community of which the citizen-voter is a part. Information about the candidate to be selected, would, the judges felt, compel the 'little man' to think over before making his choice of electing 'law-breakers as lawmakers' (*Association for Democratic Reforms* 2002). The court considered the fundamental freedom to speech and expression as commensurate with the right of citizens to know.

In recent time, epistemic communities emerging in electronic interactive domains, blogs, and social networking sites, have been seen as having the potential of making the transition to collective action. Cyberspace has presented the promise of transforming itself into fields of political action in which large numbers of 'users' communicate and connect in real time, crafting a public that transcends the regulated physical spaces of collective action. Freedom of expression has for long been seen as fundamental to the 'political morality of all democracies which profess religious tolerance and free institutions' and 'silencing' of discussion is permissible only when speech or action can harm others (Mill 1985 [1859: 73]). The surveillance regimes of the state, have, however, taken recourse to a range of techniques embedded in specific practices of rule, for harnessing, containing, and monitoring the public space. Over the years, these tools have become more sophisticated and specialized, enabling the state to reach into society in unprecedented ways, creating new and differentiated relationships of power (Singh 2014). The gathering of information about the governed was always a technique used by the state to identify problems of governance and their resolution. The modern surveillance state has emerged out of the welfare regimes of the state that required information for disbursement of welfare, and the national security regimes that crafted and honed intelligence gathering for territorial defence. While pegging itself onto the conditions of emergency precipitated by the global 'war on terror' which produce the conditions for extraordinary regimes of surveillance, the national surveillance state has become a 'way of governing' (Balkin 2008: 5) in contemporary times.

The curtailment of citizens' freedom of speech and expression has worked within the framework of 'security' and the 'reason of state', which advocates the exercise of an unrestricted panoply of powers by the state when faced with existential challenges. The security state, which emerges as a consequence of the exercise of such powers, is comprised a set of *policies* encompassing domestic security and defence against external threats, and, an *ideology* based on 'ordered liberty', whereby citizens' freedoms may be restrained to protect and promote the interests of a nation. The state invests disproportionately in the reinforcement of its security apparatus, driven by the logic of non-accountability and a culture of impunity, which manifests itself in political and legal domains. Based on the domination of its citizens, as distinct from protection from external enemies, the security state 'successfully mobilizes fear' (Young 2003: 7), submitting citizens into a protection bargain, so that they agree on constraints to their liberty and the right to dissent, and also express 'grateful love' (Young 2003: 9) towards the state for protecting them. Compelling subordinate citizenship, which is conflated with patriotism, the state expects that citizens would willingly submit and indeed participate in their surveillance, allowing the state to encroach on their privacy and freedom of speech.

The right to privacy and freedom of speech in India started diminishing with the enactment of the Information Technology Act (IT Act), 2000, which removed the two primary conditions that had to be satisfied under the Indian Telegraph Act, 1885 for justifying any infringement of the right to privacy— 'public emergency' and 'public safety'. Working on the principle of a permanent state of emergency, the IT Act amended the Indian Evidence Act, 1872, to change the meaning of 'evidence' to include electronic communication and data exchange. Chapter XI of the IT Act lists a range of 'offences', including among others, 'cyber terrorism' that carries a punishment which could extend to imprisonment for life. Section 69 of the act gave the government the power 'to intercept any information transmitted through any computer resource' in the interest of the sovereignty and security of India, its relations with foreign countries, public order, or for preventing incitement to the commission of any cognizable offence. The provisions of the IT Act ensured that the state could claim monopoly over regulating the use of cyberspace, constraining free expression within the epistemic community of digital networks and cyber commons. The ramifications of this were felt in the manner in which Section 66A of the IT Act (punishment for sending offensive messages through communication service), which was inserted through an amendment in 2009, was used to punish persons for putting up posts on social network sites. In 2012, the police in Mumbai booked a student under Section 66A of the IT Act for expressing disgust at the total shutdown in Mumbai following the death of the Shiv Sena leader Bal Thackeray. Another girl who 'liked' the post was booked along with her. This was only one of several such instances. In 2012, a young law student petitioned the Supreme Court, asking that specific sections of the act, in particular Sections 66A and 69, be removed from the IT Act for violating the constitution, in particular Articles 19, 14, and 21. Distinguishing between discussion, advocacy, and incitement, the judges construed that both discussion and advocacy fell within the freedom of speech under Article 19(1)(a) and that only incitement could attract the restraints under Article 19(2). In what has been seen as a judgement which will have a rippling effect, the Supreme Court struck down Section 66A in entirety, deciding that the section was vague, and none of the offences listed in the section fell within the purview of categories which could be reasonably restricted under Article 19(2) for the maintenance of public order (*Shreya Singhal* v. *Union of India*[2]).

Quite like the Naz Foundation and Nandini Sundar judgements, the judgement in the Shreya Singhal case can be seen as carrying forward the legacy of citizen-democracy, whereby citizens and citizens' groups become the conduits for extending rights claims by repositioning them within the institutions of the state. In 1982, in the context of the Asian Games in Delhi and more recently in 2010 when the Commonwealth Games were held in Delhi, the People's Union for Democratic Rights, a Delhi-based civil rights organization, petitioned the Supreme Court and the Delhi High Court, respectively, and drew their attention to

[2] Writ petition (Criminal) No. 167 of 2012, decided on 24 March 2015.

the violation of labour laws and various other laws pertaining to minimum wages, work and living conditions. In both the cases, the courts concurred with the petitioners and instructed the state to ensure that labour laws were not violated, and the workers not denied the benefits they were entitled to, which the court suggested was the 'least' that a government is 'expected to do in a social welfare state' (*People's Union for Democratic Rights and Others* v. *Union of India and Others*;[3] also *People's Union for Democratic Rights & Others* v. *Union of India and Others*[4]).

People's movements and campaigns run by civil society groups have increased the repertoire of enumerated fundamental and legal rights of citizens. The national right to food campaign, for example, was preceded by a public interest litigation filed by the Rajasthan People's Union for Civil Liberties, through the Human Rights Law Network in 2001. The petition drew the attention of the Supreme Court to the paradox of the overflowing godowns of the Food

[3] (1982) AIR 1473.

[4] Civil Appeal No. WP(C)524/2010, decided by the Delhi High Court on 20 September 2012.

Corporation of India, the grain rotting in the rains, and thousands of villagers in the vicinity surviving hunger and starvation by eating in turns or practising rotation eating. The court agreed with the petitioner that the right to food was a necessary component of Article 21 of the constitution to live a life with dignity, and lay down the institutional mechanisms by which the Public Distribution System and governmental schemes could be strengthened and made accessible. A National Food Security Act (2013) has sought to turn the various food security programmes of the government into statutory rights of the people.

Another illustration of how acts of democratic iteration make citizens authors of their rights, is the *jansunwai*s (public hearings) by the Mazdoor Kisan Shakti Sangathan (MKSS), and the campaign for the Right to Information Act. The jansunwais were organized by the MKSS among workers employed on government construction sites in Rajasthan. In the jansunwais the expenditure incurred by the government on specific sites was matched against the muster rolls of employment and disbursement of wages to workers. The objective of ensuring minimum wages to workers, the demand for transparency, and concerns around leakage of public money, transformed into a concerted nationwide campaign for the right to information. In a manifestation of what has been called 'jurisgenerative politics' (Benhabib 2007), whereby a democratic will is generated through deliberations and contestations in the public space, the campaign resulted in the installation of the right to information (RTI) as a legal right in 2005. The RTI, in turn, spawned vigorous activism not just around the mechanisms available within the framework of this right, but a more generalized demand for greater transparency and protection against corruption in the government.

The Insurgent Citizens

The iterative practices of democratic citizenship are reflective of the ways in which citizens' practices buttress state sovereignty by routing their activism within and through the institutions of the state. Taking recourse to the constitution for replenishing their repertoire of constitutional and statutory rights, these iterations of citizenship make the constitution a site of contestation and a domain of struggle for ascendancy between texts of governance and those of rights and justice.

Yet, people's practices of citizenship are not always about setting up interlocutory relationships with institutions of the state. They also emerge from a world beyond the struggles around constitutional text and its meaning, in a domain permeated by performative acts of the power of the state and people's resistance to the exercise of such power.

Becoming citizens by interrupting the power of the state and by refusing to participate in its rituals of ruling takes diverse forms. A literary rendition of insurgent citizenship is found in Mahasweta Devi's story '*Draupadi*'. An extract from the English translation by Gayatri Chakravarty Spivak of the story is prefaced to this chapter. A tribal woman suspected of being sympathetic to a militant, underground, left-wing resistance group, Draupadi is arrested by the police. Senanayak, the officer in charge of the operation, asks his men to extract information from her about militant activities. Draupadi is tortured and raped in custody. The next morning, when she is brought before Senanayak for further interrogation, she refuses to put on her clothes, insists on being presented before the officer in her naked state, and challenges him to kill her in an 'encounter' (Chakravarty 2009: 53).

179

By demanding that she be encountered (as distinct from being subjected to torture and rape), Draupadi erases her sexual subordination, and presents herself as a political adversary, equal to Senanayak. Quite like Bishan Singh embracing death in Manto's story '*Toba Tek Singh*', by this act of elision, Draupadi denies Senanayak the power to bring her within the purview of the state's dominative power of coercion, and control of her life and death. '*Draupadi*' and '*Toba Tek Singh*' essay a practice of citizenship, inscribing 'a moment of pure politics' as Partha Chatterjee calls it, in his description of Manto's rendition of the violence of partition and Toba Tek Singh's death. Amidst the drawing of borders and the formation of the states of India and Pakistan, the governments of the two countries decided to exchange their 'lunatics' as well. The arrangements were complete and the lists of lunatics were prepared and agreed upon. On a cold winter morning, escorted by the police, the lunatics were brought to the Wagah border. At the check-post, there was bedlam, as the lunatics bewildered and unable to comprehend the importance of the exchange operation and their sudden transformation into objects to be claimed and absorbed into one country or another, ran astray, sang, wept, or fought with each other. When it was Bishan Singh's turn to give his personal details to be recorded in the register, he demands to know where his village Toba Tek Singh was:

> ... he asked the official 'Where's Toba Tek Singh? In India or Pakistan?' The officer laughed loudly, 'In Pakistan, of course.' Hearing that Bishan Singh turned and ran back to join his companions. The Pakistani guards caught hold of him and tried to push him across the line to India.... They even tried to drag him to the other side, but it was no use. There he stood on his swollen legs as if no power on earth could dislodge him.... Just before sunrise, Bishan Singh let out a horrible scream. As everybody rushed towards him, the man who had stood erect on his legs for fifteen years, now pitched face-forward on to the ground. On one side, behind barbed wire, stood together the lunatics of India and on the other side, behind more barbed wire, stood the lunatics of Pakistan. In between, on a bit of earth which had no name, lay Toba Tek Singh. (Manto 1987)

The moment of pure politics embodied in the reclamation by Toba Tek Singh of the power to negotiate his life and death, evidently possesses an enormous potential of unleashing politics of a different kind. Chatterjee argues that this moment, while teeming with the promise of pure politics, is rendered unstable by the enormity of its promise and the burden of responsibility it places (Chatterjee 2005). Yet, as a mode of contesting both the dominative and persuasive power of the state, by emphatically recusing oneself either from becoming a receptacle of the coercive power of the state, or from consenting to its persuasive appeal and submit to its protection, 'pure politics' has reverberated in plural sites of insurgent citizenship.

Resonating the literary metaphor of Draupadi, a powerful political protest wove around the violated female body, when in July 2004, a group of women outraged at the rape and extrajudicial killing of Manorama, a young Manipuri woman, stood naked in front of the headquarters of the Assam Rifles in Manipur, challenging the army jawans to 'take their flesh'. It may be noted that the army in Manipur has complete immunity from judicial scrutiny under the AFSPA, which has been in operation in the north-eastern states of India since 1958. A continuous hunger fast since 2000 by Irom Sharmila, a Manipuri woman, demanding the lifting of the AFSPA, is an expression of citizenship through the Gandhian idiom of non-violent resistance for the reclamation of the self within totalizing regimes. The hunger fast by Sharmila presents a curious annual ritual of a cat-and-mouse game. The state attempts to bring Sharmila under the ambit of its authority by keeping her alive in its 'safe custody'. She is force-fed through a nasal tube in a hospital-prison, where she is incarcerated on the charge of attempting suicide. Each year the state releases Sharmila, who declares her intention of continuing her hunger fast, and is subsequently sent back to prison—with the life-saving, force-feeding paraphernalia reinstalled. This sequence of release, imprisonment, and force-feeding, has carried on as a perennial cycle, holding out for Sharmila and those struggling against AFSPA, an existence where they surrender and reclaim their rights to citizenship through acts of defiance against unjust laws. A rally led by women and children inserted a new chapter in the enduring struggle by the Adivasi against the setting up of a power plant in Odisha by a South Korean company POSCO. On 7 March 2013, two women in the rally led by mothers of Dhinkia and Govindpur villages in Jagatsinghpur demonstrated naked before the paramilitary station in

Mangalpada near Govindpur village, housing more than five platoons of paramilitary forces to ward off protests by the villagers against POSCO. While they took off their clothes, they constantly shouted, 'Why have you come here? What do you want to see?' (Dash 2013)

In Odisha, Gram Sabhas in successive villages in Rayagada district have rejected the proposed bauxite mining project by the Vedanta Corporation in the Niyamgiri hills held sacred by the local adivasis, reaffirming their religious, cultural, and livelihood rights over the mineral-rich hills. In Tamil Nadu, villagers and fisherfolk from the districts of Kanyakumari, Tirunelveli, and Thoothukudi, have been protesting against the Kudankulam Nuclear Power Plant (KNPP) for over 20 years. The resistance to the KNPP has taken several forms, including jansunwais and hunger fasts. People have demanded complete closure of the project on the ground that the hot water discharged from the plant into the sea will adversely affect marine life and fish catch, affecting their livelihood and impacting the environment, exposing them to the risk of radiation. All of these, they fear, would lead to the displacement of thousands of people living in the immediate vicinity of the plant. The protests have attracted disproportionate response from the state, with cases lodged against the protesters by the police, some of them on serious charges of sedition and waging war against the state. In Khandwa district of Madhya Pradesh, close to the state capital Bhopal, villagers have been performing *jalsatyagraha*, in protest against the state government's order opening the gates of the Omkareshwar dam on the Narmada river, which has resulted in the flooding of villages and damage to crops. In this unique protest, villagers, men and women, have been standing immersed in the river waters for days altogether, to assert the illegality of the order, which they argue violates the Supreme Court directive for adequate compensation and rehabilitation to villagers before water levels are raised.

While these spaces of performance of citizenship through passive resistance are far removed from the global street, they too in allied ways, as Sassen would say, make 'powerlessness complex' (Sassen 2011). The complexity of powerlessness in each of these cases may be mapped in terms of the potential it has for making radical democratic citizenship possible. A dimension of this potential also lies in the capacity of the protest to resonate in the urban street. The disruption of ritualized protest, and the eruption of radical citizen-ship in the claims made to the city space, inhabiting it with new forms of political action, may be traced in the street protests in Delhi in April 2011 and subse-quently in December 2012.

The upsurge of protests following the gang rape of a young woman in Delhi in December 2012 is an illustration of how the global street as a public world of appearance can generate enduring forms of demo-cratic citizenship. The foundation for the December 2012 protests were laid down a year before in the summer of 2011, when the India Against Corruption Campaign rallied around Anna Hazare, who sat on a hunger fast at the Ram Lila ground demanding strong and effective legal and institutional mechanisms to control and punish corruption in public offices. When Anna Hazare started his hunger fast in April 2011, he was recalling the 'saintly idiom' (Morris-Jones 1963) of Indian politics, which is conventionally seen as located 'at the margin' of Indian politics (Morris-Jones 1963). Yet, the marginality appears to be less in terms of its influence, and more in terms of the number of persons who may be personally capable of a concerted and pro-tracted performance of protest, which could galvanize public censure against the dominant political class. The importance of the saintly idiom of politics is precisely the importance the margin has for a page. There may be few or none who figure there, but the margin as a location on the page is critical as a space for comment, and for limiting and shaping the contours of the page. Sharmila's continuing hunger fast and Anna Hazare's briefer stints of hunger fasts in April and August 2011, captured the political imagination of the country at large. The selflessness which people saw in Sharmila and Hazare, was in sharp contrast to the unmasked disdain and disgust with which they perceived politics and persons in authority. The marginality of the idiom, therefore, does not correspond with the power of the idiom, and the modern elements of citizenship practices it carries with it—the power of peaceful dissent, of public spiritedness and civic conscience, and the desire for institutional integrity and trust. It is not surprising, therefore, that the euphoria generated by the hunger fast became so pervasive that it exceeded the subsidiary location allotted to it on the political page, to become a powerful political language of comment. Jantar Mantar and subsequently, the Ram Lila ground, were occupied for several days at a stretch by a mass of people cutting across class, age, caste, and ideological divides, wearing 'I am Anna' caps. The public identification with the sacrificial idiom, without actually being burdened with the requirement of enacting it personally, allowed an exponentially large numbers of persons to become participatory witnesses in Hazare's hunger fast.

Unlike Anna Hazare's sit ins at the Jantar Mantar and Ram Lila ground which conform to ritualized public spaces, the protests following the December 2012 gang rape in Delhi, demonstrated how citizens reclaim spaces wrested away from them. Initiated by the JNU Students' Union in the immediate aftermath of the rape, the protests surged in waves, taking the city administration by surprise. The protesters appeared almost like a flash mob in the heavily secured Raisina Hill area along the intersection between the North and the South Blocks in New Delhi. This area houses the national government and a ponderously powerful bureaucracy, with the President's House and the circular building of the Parliament House at two other ends, completing an imposing picture of concentration of power and authority. Having almost made it into the precincts of the President's House, the students dispersed from Raisina Hill, to congregate once again at India Gate. The region around India Gate was subsequently brought under the purview of Section 144 of the IPC, which disallows public gathering, rallies, and demonstrations. Indeed, for the purpose of qualifying as a rally, the presence of four persons is considered sufficient. Soon enough, India Gate and the adjoining Rajpath became sites with the potential of becoming India's Tahrir Square, as students, young women and men, schoolchildren, and families, made their way to it, demanding stern and immediate action from the government. The police resorted to force to scatter the crowds, using water cannons, and putting up barriers to prevent people from collecting. The city was fortified—entry into it was monitored, metro stations were shut down to make getting into central Delhi difficult for potential protesters—cumulating into security measures which were substantially more than those ordinarily put in place when the city is on high alert.

Significantly, Rajpath, which was known as the Kings Way when India was a colony, is 'a road whose name and location signal the exercise of state power' (Guha 2007: xvii). Stretching for a couple of miles from India Gate and climbing onto Raisina Hill, Rajpath is flanked on both sides by a vast expanse of green lawns, which accommodate thousands of spectators on 26 January every year to witness the annual ritual of the Republic Day. In the early years of the Republic, the Boat Club and India Gate lawns were not just the spaces where an annual display of military power and might of the state took place, but importantly, were also sites for the emergence of the public sphere. Seen in Arendt's framework, the Boat Club and India Gate lawns would embody a world of public appearance, where the immense multitude could claim Rajpath to express the desires of the janta.

This public space of appearance was, however, not entirely of the people. Periodically the government of the day and dominant political parties would lay claim to it, in a contest over competing shows of strength. In the early 1990s, a government order made Rajpath out of bounds for political rallies and demonstrations in the interest of national security and public order. Rajpath was purged of the people, and restored to the state. The tents were shifted to Jantar Mantar, an observatory in the region adjoining Connaught Place, and then again to a more constrained space at the Mandir Marg–Shankar Road crossing, where tents could come up and sit ins take place, after prior permission from the local police station had been obtained. The progressive constraining and confinement of public dissent to designated and assigned spaces, to virtually five-and-a-half yards of democracy, from the mammoth possibilities allowed by the vast stretches of India Gate and Boat Club, is symptomatic of the manner in which a security state reinforces itself through the affirmation of power by force. Perhaps the most massive of these rallies was the one called on 25 October 1988, when half-a-million farmers from western Uttar Pradesh descended on the Boat Club lawns in response to a call by their leader, Mahendra Singh Tikait. In a week-long sit in, the farmers, who came with their tractors, trolleys, carts, charpoys, hookahs, and cooking *angithi*s, converted the area into a farmer's panchayat (Damodaran 2011).

The ban on congregating at India Gate came close on the heels of the demolition of the Babri Masjid in Ayodhya in December 1992, following which the BJP decided to hold a rally at the Boat Club on 25 February 1993, to be addressed by Atal Behari Vajpayee. While it did not use the word 'ban', the government disallowed the rally stating that permission to hold it would not be given. Writing in the

191

New York Times, Sanjay Hazarika (1993) described the security arrangements that had sprung up in Delhi in the wake of the call given by the BJP. The Delhi police claimed that 2,800 people were arrested and detained in two football stadiums in the city. The Press Trust of India reported the number of arrests as higher at 5,000. In the old walled city of Delhi, which has a predominantly Muslim population, the markets remained closed, and the residents moved out of their homes to other neighbourhoods. Hazarika wrote:

> The Boat Club, a well-known center for demonstrations and other expressions of dissent, resembled an armed camp. Thousands of paramilitary troops and senior security officials, equipped with automatic weapons, riot sticks and tear gas, waited for hours under an overcast sky for a confrontation that never took place. As the day wore on, police officers from the Punjab, who were transported here for a possible violent showdown, stretched out on the lawns while paramilitary officials opened lunches of curry and rice near tents beside the stately mall known as Raj Path, which leads to Government offices. (Hazarika 2013)

The area around Boat Club was subsequently brought under a 'permanent ban', which operated through Section 144 of the CrPC, which as mentioned before, empowers a government official, including the police, to declare an assembly of four or more persons unlawful, disperse a public gathering, and allow the police to restrict public gatherings in the area for a period of 50 days. This restriction was, however, allowed to operate as a permanent ban through periodic renewals. In 2011, Bano Bi, a Bhopal Gas case victim camping at Jantar Mantar, petitioned the Delhi High Court against the operation of Section 144 as a permanent ban on holding public demonstrations in central Delhi district. The Delhi High Court ordered in the petitioner's favour, which meant that the Delhi Police could no longer operate a blanket and permanent ban by continuously renewing it. But participants in a rally would still have to seek the permission of the local police in the central district areas around India Gate, its lawns, and the adjacent Boat Club area. Thus, while the Delhi police could no longer issue a blanket ban, it could still disallow specific rallies by citing law and order problems.

In December 2012, following the protests around the gang rape, the government invoked Section 144 yet again, to make the region around India Gate and Rajpath out of bounds for the people. In the days that followed, right up to the passing of the Criminal Law Amendment Act, 2013, protesters defied the ban, claiming city spaces. In the course of the protests, the city was marked with numerous shrines—the Munirka stop where the raped woman and her friend had boarded the bus, the hospital where she was being treated, and Jantar Mantar, among several others—became points where the residents of Delhi lit candles, and held vigils. In the process what occurred was an iconization of the raped woman through her figuration as Damini (a bolt of lightning), Abhaya/Nirbhaya (fearless, another name for the Goddess Durga), Amanat (something people hold together in trust, a heritage)—each connoting a distinctive positive attribute. The simultaneity of protests in different parts of the country forged a solidarity borne out of shared outrage, mediated by social network sites and animated discussions on the television and in print media. As the nation listened expectantly to hourly updates from the police commissioner and the hospital, on the progress in the case and a corresponding decline in her health, it produced an imagined community of citizens. This community was not confined to India but encompassed Indians abroad.

In both its organized and amorphous forms, the protests demonstrated strong ideological variations, which may be seen as distributed along the fault line of the masculinist honour/izzat strand, and the feminist freedom/azadi strand. These strands invoked divergent ideas of the state—protective and dominative, respectively—which in different ways were embedded in, and arose from, the idea of security. The honour/izzat strand was perhaps best exemplified in the description of the raped woman (who was still critical but alive) by Sushma Swaraj, a senior leader of the BJP and the leader of the opposition in the Lok Sabha, as a 'zinda laash' (living corpse). Izzat/honour became a dominant slogan for a vociferous section, baying for the rapists' blood, demanding like a lynch mob that the accused be handed over to them, and asking for retributive punishments like castration, and death by hanging. This, combined with statements coming from some politicians, smacked of a masculinist camaraderie cutting across party divides and a patriarchal ownership over the authority to decide on the final course of action.

The liberation/azadi strand of protesters broadened the ambit of the protests to draw attention to some of the overarching, foundational, organizational matrices of people's lives, political, economic and social, to show how the nation state, state, communities, and citizenship are embedded in gendered hierarchies. The protesters drew attention to the foundational, reiterative, extraordinary, routine, and structural violence, which flowed into people's lives along the axes of caste, religion, language, and ethnicity. They situated the gang rape within a seamless world of normalized violence that stretched across the country—the states in north-east India, Kashmir, Chhattisgarh, Jharkhand, and Odisha, for example, where regimes of impunity operated under the impact of extraordinary laws, in the wars unleashed by the state against its own citizens, and on people protesting peacefully against dispossession of their land and resources.

Indeed, if in the honour/izzat strand the state allied tactically with the order of the family helping it to preserve its honour and reputation by bringing the family under its direct disciplinary control, the azadi/liberation strand showed that the alliance was fraught with violence, which operated as a mode of legitimation of state practices of rule, which recreated, reproduced, and reconstituted itself through sexual, caste, and communal violence. These aspects of foundational and reiterative violence made themselves manifest at diverse sites and were experienced in the lives of ordinary people—the labouring poor, the Dalit/Muslim woman, and those who dissented from the order of the family, community, and the state.

The vociferous demands for institutional intervention led to the setting up of the Justice Verma Committee, and its recommendations were received with approval by women's organizations, democratic rights groups, and civil society organizations, and lauded as the Indian Women's Bill of Rights. The Criminal Law Amendment Ordinance which was subsequently promulgated and the law that replaced the Ordinance were, however, seen as a betrayal of the expectations which the 'Verma Manifesto' as one feminist scholar called it (Baxi 2013) had raised. Another spate of protests followed, but with dwindling intensity, as the debates around the trial against the six accused, one of whom died in custody, and another as a juvenile was not expected to face serious punishment, dominated the story of the Delhi rape case.

The idea of constitutional insurgency traced by Baxi in Ambedkar's statement may be read within the framework of constitutional hermeneutics, which presents the constitution as an enduring site of contestations. These are reflected in the attempts to give the constitution a 'reflexive' as well as a 'stable' meaning in legal interpretations within courtrooms, and in the performances of citizenship outside the domain of state power, in people's practices of citizenship. It is at the interstices produced by these contestations, that the elaboration of democratic citizenship takes place. This elaboration is inspired by the possibility of constitutional insurgency, for which the constitution itself provides the tools, but is constrained by the concern around constitutional morality and durability, which puts limits on the proliferation of idioms and modes of citizenship.

The promise of democratic citizenship, it may be argued, exists in the polyrhythms of citizenship, which ultimately aim at rolling back the processes of domestication, to reclaim the 'political' in citizenship. The challenge of developing a practice of citizenship within the framework of democracy involves being conscious of the processes by which the crystallization of power at the level of political or the state takes place, which is manifest in the hegemonic articulations of citizenship. It further involves critical action whereby processes of democratization take place in the domain of the political through a progressive rolling back of structures of power. The constitutional insurgencies, which refer to the contradictions that persisted at the moment of transition from colonial subjection to republican citizenship, may be seen carrying within them the germs of insurgent citizenship. It is through the idiom of insurgent citizenship that the frontiers of citizenship can be enhanced to make it a truly momentum concept. It is important to affirm citizenship as such, especially in the contemporary context where the modern citizen seems to have moved into a zone of indifference, an individuated citizenship determined by the security state.

References

Arendt, Hannah. 1958. *The Human Condition*. Chicago: The University of Chicago Press.

Balibar, Étienne (trans. from French by James Swenson). 2004. *We, the People of Europe? Reflections on Transnational Citizenship*. Princeton: Princeton University Press.

Balkin, Jack M. 2008. 'The Constitution of the National Surveillance State', *Minnesota Law Review*, 93(1): 1–25.

Barkley-Brown, Elsa. 1991. 'Polyrhythms and Improvisation: Lessons for Women's History.' *History Workshop Journal*, 31(Spring 91): 85–90.

Baruah, Sanjib. 1999. *India Against Itself: Assam and the Politics of Nationality*. New Delhi: Oxford University Press.

—————. 2005. *Durable Disorder: Understanding the Politics of Northeast India*. New Delhi: Oxford University Press.

Basu, D.D. 1999. *Introduction to the Constitution of India*. Nagpur: Wadhwa and Wadhwa.

Baxi, Pratiksha. 2009. 'Habeas Corpus: Juridicial Narratives of Sexual Governance', CSLG Working Paper series, CSLG/WP/09/02, Centre for the Study of Law and Governance, Jawaharlal Nehru University, New Delhi.

Baxi, Upendra. 2002. 'The (Im)Possibility of Constitutional Justice', in Z. Hasan, E. Sridharan, and R. Sudarshan (eds), *India's Living Constitution,* pp. 31–63. New Delhi: Permanent Black.

———. 2008. 'Outline of a "Theory of Practice" of Indian Constitutionalism', in Rajeev Bhargava (ed.), *Politics and Ethics of the Indian Constitution*, pp. 92–118. New Delhi: Oxford University Press.

———. 2011. 'Dignity In and With Naz', in A. Narrain and A. Gupta (eds), *Law Like Love: Queer Perspectives on Law*, pp. 210–52. New Delhi: Yoda Press.

———. 2013. 'Preliminary Notes on Transformative Constitutionalism', in O. Vilhena, U. Baxi, and F. Viljoen (eds), *Transformative Constitutionalism: Comparing the Apex Courts of Brazil, India and South Africa,* pp. 19–47. Pretoria: Pretoria University Law Press.

Benhabib, Seyla. 2007. 'Twilight of Sovereignty or the Emergence of Cosmopolitan Norms? Rethinking Citizenship in Volatile Times.' *Citizenship Studies,* 11(1): 19–36.

Butalia, Urvashi. 2006. 'Migration/Dislocation: A Gendered Perspective', in Navnita Chadha Behera (ed.), *Gender, Conflict and Migration*, pp. 137–54. Delhi: SAGE Publications.

Chakravartty, Gargi. 2005. *Coming Out of Partition: Refugee Women of Bengal*. New Delhi and Kolkata: Bluejay Books.

Chatterjee, Partha. 2004. *The Politics of the Governed: Reflections on Popular Politics in Most of the World*. New Delhi: Permanent Black.

―――. 2005. 'Sovereign Violence and the Domain of the Political', in T. Blom Hansen and F. Stepputat (eds), *Sovereign Bodies: Citizens, Migrants, and States in the Postcolonial World*, pp. 82–102. Princeton and Oxford: Princeton University Press.

Chakravarty, Uma. 2009. 'Archiving Disquiet: Feminist Praxis and the Nation-State', in Ujjwal Kumar Singh (ed.), *Human Rights and Peace: Ideas, Laws, Institutions and Movements*, pp. 49–73. New Delhi: SAGE Publications.

Damodaran, Harish. 2011. 'Decline of the Farmer's Movement', *The Hindu*, 21 May, available online at http://www.thehindubusinessline.com/opinion/columns/harish-damodaran/decline-of-farmers-movement/article2035543.ece (last accessed on 21 August 2013).

Das, Veena. 1995. *Critical Events: An Anthropological Perspective on Contemporary India*. New Delhi: Oxford University Press.

―――. 2011. 'State, Citizenship, and the Urban Poor.' *Citizenship Studies*, 15(3–4): 319–33.

Dash, Minati. 2013. 'Dhinkia and Govindpur Mothers go Naked to Protest against Forcible Land Acquisition for POSCO', 15 March, available online at http://kafila.

org/2013/03/15/dhinkia-and-govindpur-mothers-go-naked-to-protest-against-forcible-land-acquisition-for-posco-minati-dash/ (last accessed on 20 March 2013).

d'Entreves, Maurizio Passerin. 1994. *The Philosophy of Hannah Arendt*. London: Routledge.

Gallie, W.B. 1955–6. 'Essentially Contested Concepts', *Proceedings of the Aristotelian Society New Series*, 56: 167–98.

Gordon, Andrew and Trevor Stack. 2007. 'Citizenship Beyond the State: Thinking with Early Modern Citizenship in the Contemporary World.' *Citizenship Studies*, 11(2): 117–33.

Guha, Ramachandra. 2007. *India After Gandhi: The History of the World's Largest Democracy*. London: Picador.

Hardt, Michael and Antonio Negri. 2005. *Multitude: War and Democracy in the Age of Empire*. New York: Penguin.

Hazarika, Sanjay. 1993. 'Fear of a Confrontation Empties Delhi's Streets', *New York Times*, 26 February, available online at http://www.nytimes.com/1993/02/26/world/fear-of-a-confrontation-empties-delhi-s-streets.html (last accessed on 21 August 2013).

Hoffman, John. 2004. *Citizenship Beyond the State*. London: SAGE Publications.

Holston, James. 2008. *Insurgent Citizenship: Disjunctions of Democracy and Modernity in Brazil*. Princeton: Princeton University Press.

IRIN (Integrated Regional Information Networks). 2011. '"Enclave" Residents Campaign for Citizenship',

23 November, available online at http://www.ecoi.net/
local_link/206171/325911_de.html (last accessed on
25 May 2015).

Kaur, Naunidhi. 2002. 'The Nowhere People', *Frontline*,
19(12), available online at www.frontline.in/static/html/
fl1912/19120600.htm (last accessed on 23 May 2015).

Kaviraj, Sudipta. 2003. 'A State of Contradictions: The Post-
colonial State in India', in Q. Skinner and B. Stråth (eds),
States and Citizens: History, Theory, Prospects, pp. 144–63.
Cambridge: Cambridge University Press.

Larson, Gerald James. 1997. *India's Agony Over Religion*. New
Delhi: Oxford University Press.

Rudolph, Lloyd I. and Susanne Hoeber Rudolph. 1958.
'Surveys in India: Field Experience in Madras State',
Public Opinion Quarterly, 22(3), 235–44.

Manto, Saadat Hasan. 1987. 'Toba Tek Singh', in Khalid
Hasan (trans.), *Kingdom's End and Other Stories*, pp. 11–18.
London: Verso.

————. 2008. 'The New Constitution', in Khalid Hasan
(ed. and trans.), *Bitter Fruit: The Very Best of Saadat Hasan
Manto*, p. 215. New Delhi: Penguin.

Marshall, T.H. 1950. *Citizenship and Social Class and Other
Essays*. Cambridge: Cambridge University Press.

Mehta, Pratap Bhanu. 2010. 'What is Constitutional
Morality?' *Seminar*, 615: 17–22.

Menon, Nivedita. 1998. 'State/Gender/Community,
Citizenship in Contemporary India.' *Economic and Political
Weekly*, 33(5): 3–10.

Mill, John Stuart. [1859]1985. *On Liberty*. London: Penguin.

Ministry of External Affairs. 2002. 'Report of the High Level Committee on Indian Diaspora'. New Delhi: Non Resident Indians & Persons of Indian Origin Division, Ministry of External Affairs, Government of India. Available online at http://indiandiaspora.nic.in/contents.htm (last accessed on 14 January 2015).

Ministry of Human Resource Development (MHRD). 1999. 'Fundamental Duties of Citizens: Report of the Committee to Operationalize the Suggestions to Teach Fundamental Duties to the Citizens of the Country', volumes 1 and 2. New Delhi: NCERT.

Morris-Jones, W.H. 1963. 'India's Political Idioms', in C.H. Philips (ed.), *Politics and Society in India*, pp. 133–54. London: George Allen & Unwin.

Narayan, R.K. 1952. 'The Election Game', *The Hindu*, 3 February.

—————. 2000. *A Story-Teller's World: Stories, Essays, Sketches*. London: Penguin.

Narrain, Arvind. 2007. 'Rethinking Citizenship: A Queer Journey', *Indian Journal of Gender Studies*, 14(1): 61–71.

Neveu, Catherine, John Clarke, Kathleen Coll and Evelina Dagnino. 2011. 'Questioning Citizenships', *Citizenship Studies*, 15(8): 945–64.

Niloy, Suliman. 2015. 'Indian Enclave Dweller's Son Prefers Living as a Bangladesh Citizen', 15 May, available online at http://bdnews24.com/bangladesh/2015/05/15/indian-enclave-dwellers-son-prefers-living-as-a-bangladesh-citizen (last accessed on 25 May 2015).

Ong, Aihwa. 2006. 'Mutations in Citizenship.' *Theory, Culture & Society*, 23(2–3): 499–531.

—————. 2007. 'Please Stay: Pied-a-Terre Subjects in the Megacity', *Citizenship Studies*, 11(1): 83–93.

Rao, B. Shiva. 1968. *The Framing of India's Constitution: A Study*. New Delhi: IIPA.

Reddy, Rammanohar. 2003. 'Citizenship with dollars and pounds', *The Hindu Sunday Magazine*, 19 January.

Sassen, Saskia. 2005. 'The Global City: Introducing a Concept', *Brown Journal of World Affairs*, 11(2): 27–41.

—————. 2011. 'The Global Street: Making the Political', *Globalizations*, 8(5): 573–9.

Sastri, V.S. Srinivasa. 1948. *The Indian Citizen: His Rights and Duties*. Bombay: Hind Kitab Limited.

Sen, Mihir Kumar. 1946. *Elements of Civics*. Calcutta: Hindusthan Publications.

Singh, Ujjwal Kumar. 1998. *Political Prisoners in India*. New Delhi: Oxford University Press.

—————. 2014. 'Surveillance Regimes in India', in F. Davis, N. McGarrity, and G. Williams (eds), *States of Surveillance: Counter-Terrorism and Comparative Constitutionalism*, pp. 42–58. London: Routledge.

Spivak, Gayatri Chakravorty. 1981. '"Draupadi" by Mahasveta Devi', *Critical Inquiry*, 8(2), Writing and Sexual Difference, Winter: 381–402.

Sriram, Jayant. 2015. 'Govt. set to grant citizenship to Hindus from Bangladesh', *The Hindu*, 11 May.

Swaminathan, Shivprasad. 2013. 'India's Benign Constitutional Revolution', *The Hindu*, 26 January, available online at http://www.thehindu.com/opinion/lead/indias-benign-constitutional-revolution/article4345212.ece (last accessed on 26 January 2013).

The Telegraph. 2013. 'SC mulls case of refugees: Apex court asks Centre & Dispur to respond to PIL', *The Telegraph*, Kolkata, 26 July.

Torpey, John. 2000. *The Invention of the Passport: Surveillance, Citizenship and the State*. Cambridge: Cambridge University Press.

Young, Iris Marion. 1989. 'Polity and Group Difference: A Critique of the Ideal of Universal Citizenship', *Ethics*, 99(January): 250–74.

————. 2003. 'The Logic of Masculinist Protection: Reflections on the Current Security State', *Signs*, 29(1): 1–26.

Index

About the Author

ANUPAMA ROY is a Professor at the Centre for Political Studies in Jawaharlal Nehru University, New Delhi, India. Her research interests straddle legal studies, political anthropology of political institutions, political ideas, and gender studies. She obtained her PhD degree from the State University of New York at Binghamton, US. She is the author of *Gendered Citizenship: Historical and Conceptual Explorations* (2013) and *Mapping Citizenship in India* (Oxford University Press, 2010), and has co-edited *Poverty, Gender and Migration in South Asia* (2008). Her research articles have appeared in various national and international journals. She was a senior fellow in the Centre for Women's Development Studies, Delhi, and has been a visiting scholar in Panjab University, Chandigarh, India;

Parson's Fellow in The University of Sydney, Australia; and visiting Professor at the University of Würzburg, Germany. She was the recipient of Sir Ratan Tata post-doctoral fellowship at the Institute of Economic Growth in Delhi and KTP Fellow at University of Technology, Sydney, Australia.